The Impact of the Career Guidance Provided by Dr. Chiagouris: Advance Praise by Former Students

"While many professors give their students contact information of recruiters and human resources representatives, Dr. Chiagouris' approach is that of a coach. He forms personal relationships with his students, learns their strengths and weaknesses, understands their passions and future aspirations and then guides his students into a career path most fitting their individual goals. "

— Marissa Rofer, Piaget North America

"Dr. Chiagouris has been instrumental in furthering the careers of countless students. His lessons transcend the universe of jobs in marketing and advertising, providing practical skills that are useful in numerous career fields."

— Anthony Reinhart, The Office of New York State Senator Andrew J. Lanza

"Dr. Chiagouris was exceptionally instrumental in helping me begin a career path right for me upon graduation. He went above and beyond by providing excellent individual guidance while I was a student at Pace University and has remained connected to me and other students post-graduation. He organizes networking events for students and is always available for any career-related advice. Dr. Chiagouris built a very unique and positive student-professor relationship."

— Anna Dudik, Booz Allen Hamilton

"Without Dr. Chiagouris' guidance, I wouldn't have known what to do after graduation. He prepared me for what to expect in the real world and was always there for me when I needed help."

— Mark Vasquez, CDMiConnect LLC

"From a former student to a young professional, I can assert that Dr. Chiagouris' advice has positively influenced who I've become. It's his enthusiasm behind providing insightful guidance that keeps recent graduates motivated when approaching this difficult job market. Any job-seeker overlooking this book is already making their first mistake."

— Jeffrey Ginzburg, 5min Media

"Dr. Larry Chiagouris helped in defining my future career. He was not only the sole professor to help me to question my goals, but was the sole *person* in my life who had the wherewithal to do so. I owe a large part of my success to Dr. Chiagouris taking the initiative to guide me on my career path."

— *Jason Sutton, LMCA*

"Dr. Chiagouris offers a wealth of knowledge and practical experience that not only allows him to expertly guide students, but also inspire them. Always willing to share his experiences, (the good, the bad, and sometimes ugly) his advice has been indispensable to me throughout my career."

— *Lauren Eriksen, Solo Group*

"Dr. Chiagouris is an educator whose job does not end at the threshold of a classroom. He strives to build a solid relationship with his pupils throughout their educational career and is consistently available for guidance even after they have bid adieu to the world of academia. It is this quality that makes him an ideal connection between his students and the world of professions and professional opportunities."

— *Bhoomi Shah, GroupM*

"He is simply amazing and represents the gold standard. Finding a job as a student without experience is a curve for which one needs a scissor to cut. I am proud to say that Dr. Chiagouris is that scissor who cuts the curve with wisdom and understanding. I will single out Professor Chiagouris as one of those few who put you down on the primrose path of success in your pursuit of a better future."

— *Olgerta Kondo, Zeppo Marketing, Inc.*

"Dr. Larry Chiagouris told me that choosing a career is a life choice so it better be one you enjoy not just something you are good at; that is the key to a successful career and a happy life."

— *Alisha Bacchus, Highland Products Group LLC*

"Dr. Chiagouris is a rare find these days. One finds that even with his heavy schedule he always makes himself available to answer questions, give advice, and discuss current events. It is no surprise that Dr. Chiagouris' manner extends beyond graduation. He is one of the few professors I have kept in touch with post graduation which is now 5 years ago."

— *Lana Voynova, Razorfish*

Praise by Readers from the First Edition

"I purchased this book as a graduation gift because the title really caught my attention and the fact that the author is a marketing professional that has worked on major accounts AND is a professor in a university made me feel that I have stumbled across the perfect gift. I know that recent college grads have the unfortunate task of overcoming the struggle to find their first job after college in a difficult job market. I think this book will help focus the graduate on what is essential to landing a job--and not repeating the typical advice that is often found in other job search books. I especially liked the chapter with the sample interview questions and answers. Chapter 3 is packed with useful info! That chapter alone was worth purchasing this book."

---Liz Franchini, Amazon Customer

"This book provides excellent 'insider info' on what it takes to get a job in today's ever so competitive marketplace. It contains very detailed tips and tricks on how to prepare for a productive job search. The book also supplies detailed questions on what to expect from prospective employers during the interview process. This intelligence is of utmost importance when you need to be on top of your game to ultimately get that dream job.
I highly recommend this book to all grads and believe that professors, too, should be marketing it to their students when they are about to enter the most crucial time of searching for a job. The advice in this book can really help these job seekers stand out in the eyes of a prospective employer."

---Alexis Verniere, Amazon Customer

"Wow!!! If you are looking for concise, useful information, this is the book. This is not another run of the mill books but offers clear, pertinent tactics to make a prospective employer want you on their team. Obviously, Dr Chiagouris is quite informed in today's job market and directs us on how to avoid common errors that frequently get our applications trashed.
His section on Resumes is very enlightening, and quite astounding. If you think all the resume software and guides are all you need, then you better re-think it. To me this section was profound and extremely valuable. If not for anything else, this section alone is worth its weight in diamonds.
I tip my hat to Dr. Chiagouris for a well thought out book, impeccably and intelligently presented."

---Joseph P. Rizzo, Amazon Customer

"The author hits the nail right on the head with this book. With his insightful words and decades of experience, you can't go wrong using his advice as a stepping stone forward into your career. Within the first few pages of the book about developing your brand, the author powerfully explains the importance of perfecting oneself in order to really flourish in the job market today. This sole piece of advice is a great foundation when going out in the job market for the first time and will surely make one stand out among its competitors. This is a great read, with helpful advice, coming from a man with years of experience in the field. You can't go wrong reading this book!!"

---Lauren Schubert, Amazon Customer

"The Secret to Getting a Job after College is the book every graduate is looking for. With the author's positive and straightforward pointers to acquiring a job, it seems as though recent graduates cannot go wrong, even in the current job market. Recent college grads will find this book relatable in every sense; the author even mentions ways to use Facebook and Twitter to one's advantage. The Secret to Getting a Job after College guides the reader through their step by step journey, from applying for jobs to sending `thank you' letters with an inspirational, yet strong voice. I highly recommend this read!"

---Alicia Scordo, Amazon Customer

"A terrific and informative read! I am the exact audience Dr. Larry Chiagouris was hoping to target with this book's content, and as a recent college grad (2008) struggling to find a job in this economic recession, I'm so glad I purchased this book!
With his senior-level experience in business marketing and teaching, Dr. Chiagouris seems to speak directly to the reader and addresses the problems we want answers too. His advice is right-on-point, and he hits all the concerns this age generation is facing. He continuously gives innovative ways to stand out and become a hot-commodity to employers seeking to hire.
I especially like how the author turns an individual into a marketing campaign. He teaches you how to become a brand, and then in-turn, how to market your brand to land that sweet job! I can't wait to put his advice in motion!!"

---Daniel Michael, Amazon Customer

The Secret to Getting a Job After College is a must read for any recent graduate looking to land a job. It is full of detailed advice and recommendations on everything from writing your resume, to phone interviews, salary negotiation, and more. The chapter about "Acing the Interview" was one of my favorite parts of the book, as the author gives invaluable guidance on everything you need to know to "sell yourself and build strong relationships". The author gives great examples of how to answer common interview questions and suggestions of what you should ask during the interview, as well. Overall, the author has brought years of experience and knowledge into writing this book and it should not be overlooked by any college graduate.

---Katherine McColley, Amazon Customer

This book is a very straight-forward and direct appeal to young job-seekers like myself. It suggests plenty of simple, yet incredibly effective, steps to increase your marketability and exposure to potential employers. Often overlooked tips, such as salary negotiation techniques and the use of power verbs in resumes and cover letters, are priceless to young job seekers. Overall, having read this book, I now pursue my employment prospects with more confidence and preparation than before. That's what the book says it will do, and it delivers. Help other customers find the most helpful reviews

---Vjollca Nikci, Amazon Customer

I received this book as a gift and was blown away. Entering the job market is intimidating and can seem like an insurmountable task once out of college. This book breaks down each step in the job-search process, from graduation to hiring, in a forward, no-nonsense way that gives the reader a crystal clear outline of how to get hired. This book was invaluable to me and offers an insiders' perspective that can mean the difference between getting the job and being passed over. If you're in college or even recently laid-off, this is the information you need to take your job-searching plan to the next level. I found the chapter discussing post-interview etiquette and techniques the most insightful. If you buy one book this year, make it this one! Help other customers find the most helpful reviews

---Jill Pfau, Amazon Customer

"*The Secret To Getting a Job After College* is the perfect step by step guide on not only what a graduate should do to get a job but what to expect after graduation. The author provides great direction for those who know exactly what they want when they graduate as well as those who have no idea what they want to do. The author also provides fantastic insight into how the minds of those hiring you will think about your candidacy for a position at their place of business. It is not always about what is written on your resume but who you are as a person. Many advisors and counselors neglect to point that out. Overall this book is a must read for anyone who is nearing graduation or has already graduated. It will not only help you get a job and the job you want, but it will also provide empowerment and confidence for your leap into the real world!"

---Casey Miller, Amazon Customer

"When you graduate college, it's obvious the next step is finding a way to pay off those loans. In the ever changing (and somewhat downtrodden) market today it's become nothing short of a gladiator competition to get your name out there to land a job that not only interests you, but makes it financially possible to make said loan payments. Enter TSTGAJAC. There are many portions of this book that seem like common sense: I am the girl that drops a handwritten thank you into a postal box as soon as I step outside after an interview. However, reading this book 3 years after graduating (and currently searching for a new job) I found many insights that had never occurred to me in marketing myself in a better light.

Written by a respected marketing professional who has been in the game for a long time, but also a university professor dealing with a new graduating class every year, the author brings a perspective to recent grads that they won't find elsewhere. The book is an easy 120 pages written in plain English with a helpful companion website full of links to aid in your job search. It's a reference book that will certainly see the wear and tear of time as you check back to refresh your memory each time you apply for a new job or go on an interview. It's not rocket science. It's the opposite: it's a necessary component to your 22 year old success."

---Amy L. Rollo, Amazon Customer

The Secret to Getting a Job after College:
Marketing Tactics to Turn Degrees into Dollars

Brand New World Publishing
333 East 80th Street
Suite 2C
New York, New York 10075

www.BrandNewWorldPublishing.com
www.TheSecretToGettingAJobAfterCollege.Com

ISBN: 978-0-9827654-2-5

Library of Congress Control Number: 2010941498

Cover Designer and Art Direction: Miao Jun Kuang
Cover Layout: Samantha Koste
Interior Layout and Back Cover Design: Miao Jun Kuang

The Secret to Getting a Job after College

Marketing Tactics to Turn Degrees into Dollars

Dr. Larry Chiagouris

Brand New World Publishing

NEW YORK, NEW YORK

To Fran, my muse in life,

to Philippa (Class of 2030),

to Mimi (Class of 2033),

and to Michael (Class of 2032).

CONTENTS

CHAPTER THREE
Acing the Interview: Building a Relationship and Selling Yourself   **118**

CHAPTER FOUR
Getting the Offer: Closing the Sale   **152**

APPENDIX

ACKNOWLEDGEMENTS

Most of the people who have worked on Madison Avenue know that great marketing ideas or highly creative advertising campaigns are rarely the work of one person. Often, one person may get the credit, but people on the team know many others contributed to the work. Such is the case with this book.

Many people deserve recognition for their contributions. The people who taught me how to teach -- my students -- have my gratitude for participating in my own development as they developed their skills with me. On the companion website to this book, many of their names appear with a big "thank you" to them all.

Members of college career services staff are often the unsung heroes in finding jobs for students. That will not happen here. During the development of the earlier edition of the book, many career services leaders at a variety of colleges and universities read the book and provided me with feedback. I want to express my appreciation for feedback received from Maxine Sugarman, and Gregorio Mendez (Pace University), Jody Queen-Hubert (St. John's University), Anne Love and Natalie Johnson (Wagner College), Marc Goldman (Yeshiva University), Julie Newman (Clemson University), Sean Gil (California State University), Kristina Sanchez (Pomona College), Kimberly Beyer (The University of Akron), Pat Nash (Central Piedmont Community College) and Jill Wesley (Harrison College). Their feedback has already influenced this edition and will also impact the next edition of the book.

In reviewing the past two years and all the research and reflection, one person served as a creative catalyst from the very beginning. Kathleen Mullen, in representing the publisher in this work, has been much more than a representative. She has been a litmus test of what was needed to make this book valuable for all students and graduates.

My parents and children have always been supportive and their support has made a difference. My wife, Fran, has been there every step of the way. Contributing her mastery of the English language with her senior experience in Human Resources, she has been the reality check every author needs.

To Fran, family, students, and colleagues: I thank you so much!

FOREWORD

This is a book very few people could write. A book about finding a job after college requires both substantial experience in industry and knowledge about the challenges of finding employment after college. I have known the author, Larry Chiagouris, for more than 25 years. He is uniquely qualified to write this book. He is both a recognized leader in the business community and in academia. His accomplishments and knowledge provide him with very special insight into what is required to succeed after college. His work shines a bright guiding light on the path a graduate should take to pursue a journey into the work force after graduation.

Given the state of our economy, the guidance in the book is of immediate value to all graduates for a variety of reasons. The objectives associated with obtaining a college education are rapidly changing. For the past 100 years, collegiate institutions have been anchored in a European influenced tradition of "education for the sake of education." While developing a well-rounded liberal arts perspective is still highly necessary to navigate today's complex world, today's environment now dictates a different focus.

We now confront an environment that challenges our quality of life. Health care, energy, security, and employment combine to form a formidable set of influences that demand a work force that will be equal to the task of achieving progress on all these issues and others that may emerge. One important factor serves as a foundation to our ability to survive and thrive as a nation: Our graduates need jobs that are equal to their skills and interests.

We must produce college graduates who can immediately contribute to our economy and the strength of our nation. Getting a job soon after graduation is no longer a desired goal – it is appropriately being viewed by students and their parents as a requirement that must be met. It is being viewed by government and progressive university leaders as critical to our future.

Getting a degree, however, is no longer a guaranteed ticket into the work force. Graduates must not only have needed skills, but they also must know how to match their skills with the most appropriate set of employers. Importantly, they must be able to convince employers they have the skills that merit a job offer. That is why this book, *The Secret to Getting a Job after College: Marketing Tactics to Turn Degrees into Dollars* is so important. It serves as an easy to understand guide for students seeking the increasingly more difficult to obtain first job out of school. Unlike the few books which have been written on this topic, this one is different. It is themed to leverage the proven marketing tactics every student, regardless of major, can immediately apply to a job search.

The first chapter provides several ideas to find the jobs that will be most relevant to a student. Every one of the suggestions in this chapter can be easily pursued to increase the chances a student will find an employment situation that is consistent with where a student wants to go with his career direction. The second chapter immediately describes all of the tactics a student can use to place their credentials in front of an employer in a manner that assures a student is viewed favorably. It recognizes that getting a job has become a competition and the tactics in this chapter increase the likelihood the student will win the competition.

Many students are not accustomed to being asked a series of tough questions over a brief period of time. In class, they may be asked a challenging question by a professor, but often, it is an isolated question and the answer that is given will not decide a student's future. In a job interview, the tough questions keep coming and coming and the answers given are crucial to a student's future. Chapter three addresses this challenge. It does it by not only providing reasonable responses to the tough questions, but by also providing a description of why the employer may be asking the questions. It provides a guide the student can use in a wide variety of interview situations.

The final chapter addresses the area students are typically least comfortable with in their interaction with employers. It takes the reader through all the steps – some of which are very delicate -- that must be addressed immediately after an interview to advance the relationship with the employer and generate a job offer worth accepting. Arranging references, negotiating a salary and turning rejection into a potential job offer are steps described in detail.

At my university – The University of South Florida Polytechnic – we have adopted a model that embraces the blend of a classic education with practical skills leading to employment opportunities. We approach the important occasion of sending off a graduation class with confidence that the students are prepared to meet the future ready to go to work. We understand, however, that while colleges may differ on what is emphasized in curriculum, one common characteristic is now shared by all. Students need to graduate and move quickly into the workplace. This book reflects the author's talent and his passion for helping students start their career in the workplace. This is a must read for every college student or graduate looking for their first or even second job. I strongly recommend it to all.

Dr. Richard E. Plank,
Director, Division of Innovation Management
College of Technology and Innovation
University of South Florida Polytechnic
Lakeland, Florida

I Would Like to Hear from You

I would like to learn about your experiences searching for a job after you have read the book. I want to know if there are specific questions that you would like addressed to help in your job search. It is of great importance to me to hear from you. Your feedback will be of help to other students and graduates because I plan to share your experiences with them.

Please send an email to me at: doctorC@thesecrettogettingajobaftercollege.com

In the email, include any of the following information:

1. If some aspect of the book helped you, please describe how it helped.

2. If you had a problem using some of the suggestions included in the book, please describe the nature of your problem.

3. If you have a question, please include the question in an email.

4. If you have a suggestion that would make the book more helpful to you and other people by making a change to future editions of the book, please share the suggestion.

Please note any comments or suggestions are greatly appreciated.

All the material received in the emails I receive will be examined and addressed. Answers to questions and the most relevant material will appear on the companion website to this book (your identity will not be revealed unless you agree to allow us to do so):

www.thesecrettogettingajobaftercollege.com/additionalhelp.html

There, I will post new information for you or I will refer you to pages on the site we have created where you will find the information. I will release the next edition of the book to reflect this new learning.

Thank you in advance for your feedback!

All my best,

Dr. Larry Chiagouris

BEYOND THE BOOK

We continue to receive helpful hints from career services counselors and readers of the book. We want to share their suggestions and updated/new material with you. Please look for links posted inside the book that will provide you with access to exclusive online content available to the readers of the book.

In addition, due to the substantial concern throughout the world about getting a job, many reporters from well known media outlets have asked me questions related to the topics in this book. They have asked me about personal branding, references, resumes, cover letters, the effective use of social networking, and a wide variety of other topics. We think that our readers should have the benefit of my answers to supplement the material in the book. To see updates reported in the media to these important topics, please go to this link:

www.thesecrettogettingajobaftercollege.com/beyondthebook

INTRODUCTION

"If you can imagine it, you can achieve it; if you can dream it, you can become it."

William Arthur Ward

Every spring, I ask the soon to graduate seniors about their plans after they finish college. These are just some of the typical responses I receive from them, many of whom are beginning to get very concerned about finding a job.

"I'm starting to get nervous."

"I'm not even sure what I'm going to do."

"I've sent out a hundred applications and I have no responses."

"My parents will kill me if I don't find something soon."

The college years for most people can be full of wonderful experiences. College life brings knowledge, new friendships, great memories, and self-confidence that those graduating can make a contribution to the world. Graduation brings an expectation that a good life is there just beyond the classroom. Getting a job, however, presents a new and sometimes unwanted sense of reality to many students. It is easy to understand that college students have a high level of anxiety as their final year of school is completed.

Few things in life are as difficult as getting that first job out of college. In a rough economy, the challenge is even greater. There is a very simple reason why it is difficult to get a job upon graduation: the vast majority of college students do not have any significant experience to leverage into an employment opportunity. Everything is even more challenging because in today's world, having a college degree no longer guarantees employment.

Although this book does not promise everyone who reads it will get a job the next day, it is designed to provide substantial assistance to job seeking students who are in college or who have recently graduated. It is created to quickly show them how to navigate the challenges that frequently occur in the journey from college to employment. It makes the process much easier.

This book is not like any other book that provides guidance on finding a job. It reflects a set of circumstances college graduates must consider upon graduation. According to a June 2007 Bureau of the Census report, approximately 3,000,000 people were expected to receive a college degree in the 2007 – 2008 academic year. If you add to these numbers the people who seek jobs after receiving a degree, a certificate, or a license from a technical school, the competition for jobs becomes challenging. If you also consider people from other countries seeking jobs in the United States, the situation becomes competitively intense. You will not be competing with *all* of these graduates for jobs in your area of interest, but you will be competing with many of them. Getting a job is a competition and you need to be equipped with the tools to win that competition.

To appreciate the tools you will need, answer this question. Did you ever wonder why some people get ahead who are not as talented as others? You may have noticed some people are not necessarily any smarter or that they do not necessarily work any harder. Yet, these very same people may get jobs or receive advantages that other more deserving people do not receive.

People who win the competition for jobs and career success know something that most people do not know. They know how to make themselves appear to be different and better than their competition. *They know how to market themselves. That is often the secret to their success. Making it easy for you to leverage that very same secret is the focus of this book.*

Graduating from a well-known school does not always translate into a job offer. Knowing how to market yourself will position you for job offers and career success. You will not have to learn all of the tools that a marketing professional knows how to use. You will, however, need the equivalent of a marketing plan to help you stand out from the competition and get a job.

This book will help you create your marketing plan. It will teach you what marketers know are effective strategies in selling products and services. You will learn how to market the most important product and that product is you. Filled with tips and strategies, this book will quickly guide you to market yourself and communicate what you have to offer to employers.

Your key to success is developing an understanding of the tactics that marketing professionals use to succeed in selling everything from cars to toothpaste to political candidates. Your market is the market of jobs and career opportunities. Throughout this book, I will share with you the techniques marketers use to succeed, and you will learn to apply these techniques to your job search.

Smart marketing always starts with an emphasis on the brand or product to be sold and discovering the potential consumers of the brand. College students seeking jobs need to understand they must treat themselves as a brand. They must assess the strengths and weaknesses of their brand and match their personal brand to the needs of a prospective employer.

Most books that address the job seeking public dance around the issue of marketing and its related tactics. Some might even assume it is an over-the-top exercise to engage in marketing to get a job. Some might conclude that the approach is too slick. However, the intense competition for jobs indicates otherwise. You need everything working for you in order to win the competition. Marketing will be one of the primary tools to get you to where you want to be.

What is different about this book is it specifically addresses the needs of college students. It is relevant for students in all majors and for both undergraduate and graduate students. To be fair, there are tens of thousands of books and articles that address the topic of finding a job. For example, I conducted a review of the book listings found in the Library of Congress database. It revealed more than 10,000 titles that contain content about jobs and careers. Very few of these books, however, include content focused exclusively on the particular needs of recent college graduates.

College students are not like everybody else. One important characteristic that distinguishes college students from other people looking for jobs is the uncertainty about their lives. Most students do not know exactly what they want to do with their lives or where they want to be in 5 or 10 years after graduation.

Not knowing what you want to do in life in precise terms is not a problem. Many people go through life never knowing exactly what they want to do. Some, who are quite sure about what they want to do with their lives after college, change their focus over time.

Most students about to graduate are excited to be on their own. They do not want to go back to mom and dad's house, where they may have to share a room with a brother or sister. Many of them will tell you they know they want a good life. Some will say that they want to make a positive difference in this world. Regardless of what they tell you, their primary objective is freedom and that starts with getting a job.

The vast majority of college students do not have much of an employment record to leverage in their quest to convince an employer they have what it takes to be worthy of being hired. I will describe ways college students can overcome any uncertainty of where they want to be and how to get past the obstacle of a limited resume.

Another point of difference of this book is its incorporation of technology-driven ideas and tactics. Technology continues to change the way we work in almost every industry and profession. It is also influencing the job search process.

A book written just 10 years ago would have referenced Internet job boards as the most technologically based innovative suggestion in support of the job search process. Much has happened in the past 10 years to move beyond job boards and websites. In each chapter, I will share with you the relevant technology-based tactics you will need to know.

The insights shared with you in this book are shaped by more than 30 years of work experience in a variety of industries. During that time, I participated in the hiring of hundreds of entry-level employees in addition to many senior managers and executives. I worked with the tech gurus at Bell Labs and Silicon Valley as well as the Madison Avenue ad people and the spin-doctor public relations professionals in New York City and California. In the course of my work, I learned which candidates succeeded in landing a job and which ended up getting a thanks, but no thanks letter. I learned the reasons for their successes and failures.

Additionally, my insights are influenced by my service as a Professor of marketing. I have been teaching students marketing at the undergraduate, graduate, and doctoral level for more than

20 years. For the past eight years, I have been teaching at Pace University as a full-time member of the faculty. During my time as a professor, I have had the opportunity to counsel my students about how to obtain and then keep their first job out of school. Their feedback has helped me fine-tune my advice to the newest group of graduates. The readers of this book will receive the benefit of that experience.

In addition to real world experience and collegiate teaching, I have conducted up to the minute research with specialists in the hiring arena. To enhance the knowledge shared with you, I have interviewed career counselors within and outside of collegiate settings. I have also conducted interviews with human resource managers and specialists at employment agencies. Their recommendations have sharpened my sense of what you will need to know to provide you with valuable tools throughout this book.

In Chapter One, "Finding Your Job: Identifying Your Best Opportunities," I briefly summarize key sources of information you can use to decide how to focus your job search. I examine the myth of what kind of job a college graduate should look for and I help you through the maze of specific options available to find the jobs you want.

Once you have targeted the companies you want to work for, you will need materials and tactics to attract and keep the attention and interest of potential employers. In Chapter Two, "Getting the Interview: Creating Your Marketing Campaign," I describe a recommended approach to creating your cover letter and resume as well as web-related tactics. The insights I share with you in that chapter focus on getting you to the top of an employer's list of candidates and keeping you there.

I will guide you on developing a plan to enhance your marketing efforts. That plan involves the creation of your brand and importantly, your brand positioning. Professional marketers focus on conveying what makes their brands different and better than the competition. You will need to do this too and I will provide guidance how to do it and how to use it.

Only you can make the sale when you speak directly with employers. Chapter Three, "Acing the Interview: Building a Relationship and Selling Yourself," provides you with all you need to know to make it through almost any interview situation. I will coach you how to answer the occasional tricky questions that interviewers toss at you. You will be viewed as a serious candidate for a job by learning key interviewing etiquette.

Chapter Four, "Getting the Offer: Closing the Sale," provides you with the information you will need to get an attractive offer from an employer. It also provides tips to be sure you are well positioned for the future. It includes suggestions to stay in contact with prospective employers in a professional manner after your initial contact with them. You will learn tips on salary negotiation and how to increase the chances that there will be another job for you almost immediately after you start your first job. Whether it is moving up the ladder within the company you join or moving to a better job at another company, you will be coached to assure you have employment beyond that first job.

The objective of this book is to be the one place to go for quick and easy answers to all your job search questions. I designed it this way because I know you do not have a lot of free time. Most people never see college life up close after they have graduated. They may forget how little free time is available to a typical college student.

Many people think college students have enormous amounts of leisure time. They think a typical college student hangs out in a café before returning to his dorm room to play video games or prepare for an evening of all night partying. Now I know that there is a lot of café coffee drinking, video game playing, and all night partying by many college students. The problem with this narrow view of college life is that it excludes a large number of students who are not focused on drinking/playing/partying. Certainly, most students don't engage in that kind of activity on a daily basis, particularly as they enter their senior year.

Students are time pressed seeking to accommodate several activities simultaneously. Their daily grind includes going to classes, doing group projects and term papers, studying for exams and perhaps trying to raise their grade point averages to make up for a bad semester earlier in their college career. They also have many more activities beyond academics going on in their world.

Most students have one or two part-time jobs and some have a full-time job. They are active in clubs or sports, engaged in some kind of social life and yes, they usually have to do their own laundry and handle their own living arrangements in a dorm room or apartment without many amenities or services. Along the way, many students volunteer their time to worthwhile causes and seek to squeeze in the occasional trip home or phone call to grandma or grandpa. They have no time to spare! That is why this book has been designed to be a one-stop shop for all they need to know about getting a job.

There is no need to add another 300-page textbook to a student's backpack. To keep the information I share with you convenient and current, I have provided links in the book to pages on a website created for the readers of the book. The material on the website includes references to many other job search resources, including links to several helpful websites and resume examples for a variety of majors.

If you have the time to immerse yourself in reading other books on the job search topic, I strongly encourage you to do so. To help with that task, I have created a bibliography on the topic of getting a job and careers in general. It is in the appendix. Most of the books included in the bibliography are in the bookstore provided by the National Association of Colleges and Employers (NACE). I am a member of this organization. It is an organization dedicated to assist college graduates in finding their way in the world of work. I added book titles to the list beyond the NACE bookstore to provide you with additional information to guide your career planning.

Although I will use the term "company" when referring to prospective employers, that term is a general reference to all employers. All tactics and tips shared with you are relevant for all organizations. If you are interested in working at a nonprofit organization, governmental body, educational establishment or healthcare-related facility, this book will help you find your way to a job at those kinds of employers as well.

Now, let's get a job!

CHAPTER ONE

Finding Your Job:
Identifying Your Best Opportunities

"The richest people in the world look for and build networks,
everyone else looks for work."
Robert T. Kiyosaki

You have worked hard over the course of your college career, spending long nights preparing for tests, or writing papers. You probably did a fair amount of partying, concert going, and staying out all night. That's OK. It's perfectly normal to have some fun too. It's time, however, to turn all that work and fun into a career. Developing your personal brand is one of the first steps in getting your career started.

DEVELOPING YOUR PERSONAL BRAND

Successful marketers usually conduct intensive assessments of the brand or product they are selling. They study the perceptions of the customers they want to reach in order to understand how customers perceive their company and how they want customers to perceive them. A brand is a name or term associated with a product. A brand reflects a symbol or idea that the product seller seeks to associate with a product.

Ultimately, a brand expresses a level of quality to potential customers. Assessment by marketing professionals usually centers on matching a product with a target audience. Of the many brand-related cues and symbols that they can choose to develop and emphasize, they seek those most appealing to their target audience. By doing this, marketers can expect to get the highest return on their strategy and investment in time and dollars.

These marketing practices apply to college graduates entering the work force. You need to sell your skills and time to prospective employers. Your goal is to convince employers to buy your product—*you*—and give you a job. Why should they hire you? To answer that question, you need to do what marketers do. You need to focus with laser-like precision on defining your brand and developing your brand positioning. Let's review what this marketing speak is all about.

Your personal brand is a composite of many qualities about you. It reflects areas such as how you dress, speak, carry yourself, and treat other people. The things you are known for are elements of your brand. When people say, "She is a hard worker," "He never gives up," "She is reliable," or "He is very kind," these characteristics contribute to a person's brand definition.

Employers appreciate having a job candidate with a well-defined personal brand. The NACE website provides tips about how to develop a strong personal brand. On the NACE website, the national recruiting brand and communications manager for PricewaterhouseCoopers LLP, Kitsy Blanc states, "One of the common mistakes students make is not truly understanding what a personal brand is. It's an uncomfortable situation when a recruiter asks a student to tell her about himself and the interview comes to a halt."

Having an explanation about why your brand is better than other available brands is key to your brand positioning. Creating and communicating your brand positioning is one of the most important steps you will take in planning your search for employment. It is as crucial as developing a cover letter or resume. It is far more important than figuring out how to navigate the help wanted ads. Branding is something you must work on immediately because it impacts so many of your job search activities.

Marketers differ slightly how they go about positioning the product they are selling. Regardless of their individual approach, smart marketers know that strong positioning requires identifying three major areas:

1. the product
2. what it does and its attributes and benefits
3. how it is better than the competition

Putting this strategy to work in terms of seeking a job, you need to identify and express who you are as a brand; what you are offering (your skills and education); and how you are better than the competition.

Several reasons compel a successful job candidate to have a carefully developed brand positioning. First, when you meet someone who might be helpful to you in your job search, how will you direct her attention? How do you want people to perceive you? When you look at the job specifications in an ad online or offline, which of these ads best match your skill set? When you send a cover letter and resume to an employer, what key message do you want to convey in these critical materials you send to employers? Your overall brand positioning will shape the answers to these questions.

In developing your brand positioning, you can borrow an approach from the people who have made the process integral to their profession. You can borrow from the television show Ad Men and the advertising industry. One of the most famous advertising men of the last 100 years is David Ogilvy, founder of Ogilvy & Mather, an international advertising and marketing agency. It is often said that he constantly looked for a competitive edge that he could use to sell his clients' products. One of his more famous campaign slogans was *"Only Dove is one-quarter moisturizing cream."* Notice how this single, short sentence captures all three major areas of a strong product positioning.

Another brand I was engaged to assess is BMW. This is a brand that represents high performance in the minds of many people. Importantly, the brand slogan *"The Ultimate Driving Machine"* has contributed substantially to carving out an identity in the minds of its prospects. There are many other examples beyond Dove or BMW, but you can learn from these examples that developing a strong positioning allows others to immediately see you in a way that is different from the way your competitors are viewed.

Developing a strong positioning is not rocket science but, it cannot be accomplished in 5 minutes. It requires some concentrated effort. People who have worked for David Ogilvy have told me he instructed his staff to "Interrogate the product until it confesses to its sins." What he meant is the brand manager must analyze all that the product has to offer to find the one message that can become the basis of a marketing campaign. You are the brand manager of your campaign. You too must analyze and assess who you are and what you do well.

You can expect to communicate your brand with prospective employers. You also can anticipate that potential employers will want you to share your narrative or brand story—the parts of your life that make you unique, interesting, and set you apart from other candidates.

As you progress further in the job search process, people interviewing you will want to know what motivates you. They might be interested in knowing general things about you such as where you were born and where you grew up. Expect to share this kind of information with them in a way that is consistent with your brand positioning.

Developing your brand positioning does not require you go off in the woods like Henry David Thoreau and meditate while becoming one with nature. You don't have to meet with yogis in the Himalayas to search for truth and light. This positioning task is far easier than a "Why am I here and what is the meaning of life" exercise. You simply have to know what sets you apart from other people so employers appreciate the advantages you offer them compared to other candidates.

Part of this process requires defining and developing a brand that is consistent with your goals and objectives. Marketers call the result a "brand vision statement." New job candidates also need to have a brand vision.

Newly graduated student brands are often a work in progress. You can shape perceptions about who you are and about your brand so that these perceptions are consistent with your goals. You cannot totally control the future, but you can direct your efforts toward consistency with your values and goals.

Many job seekers benefit from developing a Personal Vision Statement for themselves before writing a resume. A Personal Vision Statement can assist in bringing focus to your goals and your brand. These are not long essays or term papers. Rather, these Personal Vision Statements are one to two pages with information about what is important to you. Ask yourself questions that will lead to answers that provide a foundation for your Personal Vision Statement. Typical questions include the following:

1. How do I want to spend a typical day at work?
2. What do I value most: money or security?
3. What talent do I have or can I develop to use in my job?

The shorter and more focused the statement the better it serves as a guide to your career choices. Here are examples of focused Personal Vision Statements:

An Education major may have this vision:

To obtain experiences and advanced education in teaching so I can change the lives of students.

A Journalism major may have this vision:

To become a leader in the news industry and advance the sharing of knowledge about government and economic policies.

A Nutrition major may have this vision:

To become an expert on nutrition related issues impacting women and contribute to better understanding of nutrition practices in poor countries.

To define your brand early in your process, answer the following questions. What makes you different? What makes you better? What are you good at doing? What is the key message or impression you want to leave with other people after they have met you in person, on the telephone, or online?

Think about what evidence you have to support your answers to these questions about what makes you different and better. Marketers refer to this evidence as "reason to believe." All of these questions focus on coming to a conclusion about the advantages you bring to any job situation that can be a basis for convincing people to hire you.

If you are not sure of the advantages you bring, consult with people who know you well. Ask them to help you identify your strengths. Meet with professors whose classes you have taken, and employers for whom you have worked or interned. Weigh most heavily the input you get from people who know you well and can provide an objective point of view. Please be cautious in obtaining feedback from those who love you. They are too close to you, and their perspective is influenced by how much they care about you. As a result, their evaluations may not be objective.

There are many tools and guides available to help you navigate the process of defining your brand. One popular book on the subject is *StrengthFinders 2.0*, authored by Tom Rath. Based on work developed by the Gallup organization, it provides tools and strategies for identifying and applying your strengths.

You do not have to arrive at a brand positioning that indicates you are the best in the world at something you do. You just have to be viewed as better at it than most other people. You need to know what you like and what you are good at. Armed with that point of view, you will be able to convince others you not only know where you are going, but also that you know the value you offer. You can focus your communications with others on the strengths you will bring to employers if they hire you.

A well-developed description of your brand positioning is an important element of what you share with people when you meet them. It sets the stage for how to engage people and for your discussions with them. Keep in mind, someone who is a networking contact or a new acquaintance requires less information than a potential employer. What you share with potential employers needs to contain more information, including who you are, what you do, and *why you are better* than other people who may be under consideration for the same job.

Here is an example to help you think through the process so that you can learn how to convey your brand positioning to others. Imagine you are a Journalism major graduating from Syracuse University. Imagine you are in a professional setting where you are introduced to people who can help you with your job search. Graduating as a Journalism major presents its own challenges because it is a popular major, and Journalism is a highly competitive field. As a result, you want to say more than, "Hello, I'm Nancy Smith." You may not have an opportunity to speak to this person again, so you need to share more about yourself. Try to engage the person and get a conversation going in a relationship-building direction. Try to ensure the other person knows what kind of work interests you. You could say, "Hello, I'm Nancy Smith, I'm a Journalism major graduating from Syracuse."

If you sense there is an opportunity to provide more detail about yourself, you should take advantage of it. I recommend you share something about yourself that reveals your special interests or skills beyond your college major. Shape your description of who you are and your experience to fit with what you think the people you are speaking with will find interesting.

An important difference between a personal brand and a commercial brand is that a personal brand has many more dimensions. People are complex and possess a variety of interests and skills. These interests and skills all contribute to the composition of a personal brand. Provide information relevant to your personal brand that reflects the interests or skills that are the best fit for a particular conversation. For example, if you're speaking with people looking for a Journalism major to cover stories for a health column (and you have an interest in and some knowledge about health), you can add "with an interest in health-related news stories." The complete description in this example would be "Hello, I'm Nancy Smith. I'm a Journalism major graduating from Syracuse with an interest in health-related news stories."

Of course, be prepared to back up that statement with possible answers to subsequent questions that emerge in the conversation. All of the communications about who you are must be supported by reality and based on attributes you possess. By grounding the expression of who you are in facts you can support, you will feel more confident in discussing yourself with others and you will be better able to engage in any questions about your background.

The value of going beyond sharing your name is it provides you and the other person with a comfort zone in terms of topics for discussion. Health care news as a topic in this example serves as a jumping off point that allows you and the other person to move immediately into a deeper conversation about something you both find of interest. By providing more information about yourself that is relevant to your personal brand, you have a great way to begin building a relationship.

Taking it to the next level, you should consider providing more detail about your experience and qualifications to add more specific information about your brand. Your goal is to include additional information that conveys to interested people that you are better than those competing with you for the job. You are not going to use the exact words, "I am better" because that might be viewed as arrogant. However, you do need to say something that will tell people you are special in some way.

Returning to the Journalism major example, you could add, "I am one of the few recent graduates who has experience working on health-related content both in the classroom and in the field. Many of my investigative reporting experiences, internships, and term papers have focused on health-related topics." This statement, which reflects a brand positioning, immediately sets a job candidate apart from the competition.

If you do not have specific experience, you can start right now to acquire the experience you need to differentiate yourself from other job candidates. Apply for an internship or volunteer to help a worthwhile cause in your community. What matters is obtaining credible skills and experience while you continue to search for the job you want.

Former students contact me after graduating saying they now have a newly acquired passion for a subject area, but no experience in it. They ask me what to do. My recommendation is to start interviewing experts in their field of interest and start blogging about the subject and what they have learned. These activities are likely to provide a student with experience and knowledge, writing samples, contacts, and name recognition. Of course, if you are going to blog, you should be certain you have something to say. If you have a passion or interest in an area, you will most likely have a lot to say and again, that will set you apart from the competition.

You will find many occasions when you have only 10 or 20 seconds to share with someone who you are. Sharing your brand positioning in a crisp and easy to understand manner takes practice. It helps to be able to practice in increments. Practice saying it in 10 seconds. Practice adding additional detail that describes who you are and then saying it in 20 seconds. Communicating your brand positioning briefly is great practice. It is called an *elevator speech* because it is done quickly, in the time it takes an elevator to go just a few floors. It will be the most important speech you can make.

While the "elevator speech" length is the most common basis for introducing yourself, you also may find occasions when you have more time. Prepare yourself so you can deliver a 20 to 30 minute discussion about yourself if the employer provides you with that amount of time. Give substantial thought as to where you would take the opportunity to describe yourself to other people. When you do have more time, you should be prepared to take it with further details, facts, and specifics to back up your brand positioning.

Chapter Two provides a reference to material other students or recent graduates are using to convey their respective personal brand on the Internet. As you work to develop your personal brand, remember you will need to update it regularly. How you think of yourself and how you want others to think about you will change. You need to be confident you are in command of your personal brand and its expression by continuing to refine it and maintain it.

FOCUSING ON OPPORTUNITIES TO PURSUE

Once you have developed your elevator speech, you need to focus on which opportunities to pursue. There is no set number of opportunities to pursue. If you are not selective, including too many job possibilities, you may waste time and get discouraged when you find that you are not getting callbacks. However, if your focus is too narrow, you could be omitting those opportunities on the path not taken. You could be missing an entirely new direction in life.

My recommendation is to err on being too broad in your search unless you definitely think you know exactly what you want to do, where you want to do it, and where you want to work. If you are a person who knows exactly what you want to do in life immediately after college, you are fortunate. You may be able to skip to the next chapter. However, even with your great focus, you might want to validate your goals by reviewing material in this chapter because it may refine your direction.

The way to proceed in identifying your opportunities is first to decide what your geographic boundaries will be. You need to decide which areas of the country (or for that matter, which areas of the world) are of interest to you and which areas you wish to avoid. Marketing professionals usually start with a broad definition of their target audience and then narrow it after further analysis. You should do that too.

Anywhere you go geographically might only be for a year or two. You can always move on to somewhere else when you think you are ready for a change of scene or want to return home. Nothing has to be permanent. Often, some of the best professional moves are to unattractive places where there is less competition for jobs. Try not to limit your geographic boundaries. The wider the boundaries, the more opportunities you can find.

DETERMINING POTENTIAL INDUSTRIES AND PROFESSIONAL DISCIPLINES: THE MYTH

Once you decide on geography, you will need to determine which industry sectors and/or professional disciplines are relevant to your search. Many recent graduates think they are more limited than they really are. However, this could not be further from the truth. They limit themselves to only the job opportunities that are highly relevant to their major. *It is a myth that a student should only pursue opportunities in his academic major.*

College trains you to think and communicate. While in college, you may learn many of the skills that are specific to a particular profession. Success at most entry level jobs requires analytical and communications skills more so than mastery of content associated with a particular college major. Most employers know that a wide variety of majors can satisfy their entry-level requirements. The deciding factors in choosing an employee are often the employer's perception that the job applicant communicates effectively and will be able to learn the job responsibilities quickly.

Exceptions do exist. If you do not speak Spanish, there is no chance you will accompany the President as one of his interpreters on his next visit to South America. Of course, if you have never had an accounting course, you are also not likely going to be hired as an auditor at the IRS – or at least, I hope you are not be hired as an IRS auditor. Keep in mind that the exceptions are not the rule.

Don't be too narrow selecting opportunities of interest to you. Think as broadly as possible. It will increase your chances of uncovering employment situations that can take you in new directions. These could become exciting career paths you may not have thought about when you first began your job search.

DETERMINING YOUR POTENTIAL MARKET

Marketers use a variety of techniques to determine the market size for their products. They identify the most relevant target audiences and then shape communications directed to the target audiences in a way that meets their needs. You can do the same thing. You can determine the size of a market for your services and shape your communications to fit the target audience's needs.

Deciding which types of jobs to pursue is an important step in establishing priorities. Some students are tempted to chase every opportunity they learn may be available. The problem with this approach is it lacks focus and is inefficient. You may end up wasting time instead of focusing on opportunities most in line with your career interests and skill set.

There are several ways to narrow your job and industry search. You should start by meeting with the people at your college who work in the career services department. You should do this as early as possible in your college career. These are professionals trained to help you focus on the jobs best suited for you based on your interests, skills, and experience.

If you have already graduated, don't despair. In most cases, the college career services staff members are still willing to help you identify opportunities. Many colleges offer free or low-cost services to help you assess your areas of interest and skill. You should use these services to help you focus your search on opportunities that are relevant to what you can and should do with your career.

College career counselors are often among the most dedicated college employees. They are passionate about helping students. They care about your success. Many are members of the National Association of Colleges and Employers (NACE). The NACE mission is to facilitate the employment of the college educated. Its members are clearly people you should speak with when given an opportunity to do so. In Chapter Two, we will review how to work with career services professionals so that your time is used most effectively.

Most students succeed in areas where they have a strong interest and have relevant skills. To help students narrow their focus, I have them conduct an easy to do exercise. We develop a list of jobs that they might consider. I ask students to rate jobs on a scale from one to ten. I ask them to rate themselves in terms of how interested they are in these jobs. I then ask them to indicate how skilled they think they are in terms of doing these jobs.

Jobs that reflect high levels of skill or interest should get scores of seven through ten on each of those aspects. Jobs that reflect low levels of skill or interest should get scores of one through four. Of course, you can rate a job at any level, including five or six, but the objective here is to avoid middle of the road compromises. The exercise results in the development of a

Skills/Interests Grid. The sample on the following page provides you with the format to create your own grid.

Various types of jobs can be categorized into one of the four priority boxes reflected in the grid. Jobs that a student is particularly interested in and for which he has the right skills are placed in the upper right hand corner of the grid. These jobs should get serious consideration and given top priority. These jobs should be the focus of a job search. Jobs in the upper left hand corner or lower right hand corner have only one relevant quality. These jobs should get modest consideration and given a lower priority. Finally, jobs in the lower left hand corner should be avoided – searching for them is not the best use of your time. These jobs should receive the lowest priority.

There are always challenges with this exercise. Some students tell me they are interested in everything. Regardless of your interest level, you have to set priorities to make the best use of your time. As you work through the grid exercise, keep yourself disciplined and set priorities. You may be interested in everything, but drill down until you come to terms with what interests you most.

What if you do not have a great interest or passion in any one direction? Don't worry about that. You're in good company. Many highly successful people were unsure about what they wanted to do when they graduated from college. In fact, the most well known management consultant of the past century, Peter Drucker, often commented about his interests and goals in life. At age 58, he was quoted in a *Psychology Today* article in which he stated that he did not know what he wanted to do when he grew up!

Some people go through life changing their focus and pursuing new dreams. It is quite common to do so and you will have many opportunities to change your goals too. If you don't have a passion at this moment, you may have some things that interest you more than others. Look for jobs in those areas of greater interest and a passion may develop.

SKILLS/INTERESTS GRID

High

S
K
I
L
L
L

Priority #2:	Priority #1:
Give modest consideration to these jobs.	Give serious consideration to these jobs.
Priority #3:	**Priority #2:**
Avoid these jobs.	Give modest consideration to these jobs.

Low ←————— INTEREST ————→ High

As you narrow your focus, you can gain a better understanding of the possibilities available to you from some highly respected sources. I often direct students to two studies that provide a great overview of career opportunities. One study is published by *Money Magazine* and can be found at www.money.com/bestjobs. The other study is published online by CareerCast at www.careercast.com. These sources have been available free on the Internet and provide helpful information.

The *Money Magazine* study is based on an analysis of work performed by PayScale.com. It combines a variety of data sources from reputable organizations including the United States Bureau of Labor Statistics, the Conference Board Help Wanted Online Series, and research by the *Money Magazine* staff. The result is a publication that provides details concerning the top 50 jobs in America, including growth rates, job descriptions, and comments from people who currently have these jobs.

The CareerCast research examines 200 jobs. CareerCast is owned by Adicio, Inc., in which *The Wall Street Journal* owns a minority interest. CareerCast rates each job on several criteria. The job environment (work conditions), income, outlook for growth, stress on the job and physical demands related to the jobs are criteria included in the rating system.

The table on the following pages provides a list of the rankings of the top 50 jobs assessed from both rating systems.

Rank	*Money Magazine*	CareerCast
1	Software Architect	Actuary
2	Physician Assistant	Software Engineer
3	Management Consultant	Computer Systems Analyst
4	Physical Therapist Nurse Practitioner	Biologist
5	Environmental Engineer	Historian
6	Civil Engineer	Mathematician
7	Database Administrator	Paralegal Assistant
8	Sales Director	Statistician
9	Certified Public Accountant	Accountant
10	Biomedical Engineer	Dental Hygienist
11	Actuary	Philosopher
12	Dentist	Meteorologist
13	Nurse Anesthetist	Technical Writer
14	Risk Management Manager	Bank Officer
15	Product Management Director	Web Developer
16	Healthcare Consultant	Industrial Engineer
17	Information Systems Security Engineer	Financial Planner
18	Software Engineering/Development Director	Aerospace Engineer
19	Occupational Therapist	Pharmacist
20	Information Technology Manager	Medical Records Technician
21	Telecommunications Network Engineer	Sociologist
22	Environmental Health & Safety Specialist	Stenographer/ Court Reporter
23	Construction Project Manager	Medical Secretary
24	Network Operations Project Manager	Bookkeeper
25	Emergency Room Physician	Astronomer

Rank	Money Magazine	CareerCast
26	Information Technology Business Analyst	Economist
27	Director of Nursing	Physicist
28	Information Technology Consultant	Dietitian
29	Psychiatrist	Parole Officer
30	Test Software Development Engineer	Medical Technologist
31	Information Technology Network Engineer	Motion Picture Editor
32	Senior Sales Executive	Geologist
33	Information Technology Program Manager	Civil Engineer
34	Primary Care Physician	Computer Programmer
35	Computer and Information Scientist	Industrial Designer
36	Hospital Administrator	Petroleum Engineer
37	Programmer Analyst	Medical Laboratory Technician
38	Applications Engineer	Occupational Therapist
39	Research & Development Manager	Insurance Underwriter
40	Regional Sales Manager	Purchasing Agent
41	Project Engineer	Physiologist
42	Training Development Director	Nuclear Engineer
43	Human Resources Consultant	Audiologist
44	Speech-Language Pathologist	Broadcast Technician
45	Business Development Analyst	Market Research Analyst
46	Physical Therapy Director	Librarian
47	Structural Engineer	Anthropologist
48	Nursing Home Director	Architectural Drafter
49	Systems Engineer	Vocational Counselor
50	Healthcare Services Program Director	Archeologist

In reviewing the list, you might be wondering why the rankings are so different. Here is a reason: the two systems differ in the criteria used to rank the jobs and in how much importance they assign to each of the criteria. This is not an unusual set of circumstances. No two people have the exact same values as to what they want out of life. Similarly, two highly respected organizations can produce two different sets of rankings.

The best way to use these rankings is to read the original material online to determine for yourself what meets your needs. This quick research step will improve your ability to narrow your focus. Here is an opportunity for you to reflect on what is important to you. You may not mind being in a stressful situation if it brings you high growth potential. On the other hand, you may prefer to avoid stress and are less concerned about income. Exploring the CareerCast and *Money Magazine* material will help you identify what is important to you.

IDENTIFYING POTENTIAL EMPLOYERS

Deciding on geography and industry sectors are the first two steps in finding opportunities that match your brand/product. The third step is identifying potential employers within the geographic areas and industry sectors that interest you. You have to develop what we refer to as "leads." Leads are the lifeblood of direct marketing and sales professionals. Many leads have to be generated in order to make a sale. The same is true when looking for a job. You will need to develop many leads in order to get the job that is a good fit for you.

Before providing you with tips to generate leads, you will notice that I have not yet discussed Internet job boards or help wanted ads in the newspaper. Although these are important sources of leads, tapping into the "hidden job market" is likely to generate more leads for you. I will share my thoughts about job boards and help wanted ads later in this chapter. First, let's focus on the far greater potential presented by the hidden job market.

Estimates suggest that the majority of all jobs are NOT advertised. Jobs that are available but not advertised are referred to as part of the hidden job market. There are many reasons employers rely on the hidden job market, including saving the cost of advertising, preventing the receipt of unwanted resumes and avoiding extensive screening processes. At the entry level, a deluge of resumes arriving every day at an employer's business may be the main reason an employer avoids advertising its jobs. Therefore, you need to generate your leads from sources beyond ads on the Internet or in the newspapers.

JUMPSTARTING YOUR LEAD GENERATION PROGRAM: NETWORKING EVENTS

To jumpstart your own lead generation program, you should attend networking events. These events may be conferences, conventions or even academic and professional programs conducted at your college or at colleges near you. Local merchant organizations, professional societies, trade organizations, chambers of commerce, and even houses of worship also arrange networking events.

You will meet a wide variety of people at networking events. Some of the people you will meet may be hiring employees or may know of other people who are seeking to add staff to their organizations. Now that you have sharpened your focus as to the kind of jobs you find of interest, you can use that knowledge to more effectively allocate your time spent at networking events. Clearly, if you have a particular industry or job in mind, you can seek contact with people at a networking event who might help you identify a job lead in your desired field. You can attend industry events focused on employers in your area of interest.

There are no hard and fast rules for making the most of a networking encounter. Some of my suggestions below are based on extensive experience attending networking events. I have observed that many people don't make the most of a networking event. Here are some tips to be sure that you are successful:

1. Dress for success. That means do not attend a networking event dressed too casually. Chapter Three covers how to conduct a successful interview. That chapter includes guidance on what to wear when you go on an interview. The key thing to remember is that it is better to come slightly overdressed than poorly dressed. Always bring a briefcase with you. It will enhance your image as a professional.

2. Read "Shut up and Listen," a section in a book entitled *The Power of Nice* by Linda Kaplan Thaler and Robin Koval. In their book, the authors make a great point about building relationships. They recommend that you speak less and listen more. Be sure you follow that advice when you attend a networking event. Let the people you meet do most of the talking. You will learn more that way and they will probably appreciate you more because you listened.

3. Work as much of the room as time allows. That means you need to approach as many people as possible and introduce yourself to them. I know many people just starting out find it difficult to introduce themselves to total strangers. If it comforts you, you should know that even highly accomplished and experienced people remain apprehensive about introducing themselves to strangers. However, the more often you do it, the less uncomfortable you will become. This is a good time to get started and gain that experience.

4. Have your personal brand positioning and your brand story ready to share with others. When someone asks you what you do or why you are at the event, be prepared to answer those questions in a way that communicates your brand positioning. Be ready to go beyond the elevator speech version of it, taking it to a greater level of detail that will position you the way you want to be perceived.

5. Unless a conversation is going very well, you should try to limit your discussions with each person to between 5 and 10 minutes. At the end of a conversation, tell the person that it was nice to meet them and offer your business card to them. I will discuss how to create a business card for a student or unemployed graduate in Chapter Three. Be sure to get the other person's business card. Immediately after meeting the person, jot some notes on the back of the card that reflect information to help you remember the person the next time you make contact.

6. Avoid the mistake of treating a networking event as a dating situation. Do not use the time to meet a potential date. This is a common mistake made by people new to networking. Focus on why you are at the event—to get a job.

7. Do not be overly aggressive at a networking event. Remember that your primary goal is to meet new people and to develop your contact list. If someone asks for a copy of your resume, you should certainly provide it. Don't pull it out of your briefcase unless someone asks you for it.

8. Look for opportunities to follow up with your new contacts. Sending your new contacts an email indicating that you enjoyed meeting them is a good idea. If during

the course of your conversation, you learned that a person you met has an interest in a particular topic and, subsequently you learn something new that is relevant to that topic, a brief email to that person sharing the information will assure you will be remembered.

College career fairs are another major source of leads. These fairs are common at every college and university. My own university, Pace University, conducts several of these throughout the academic year. Here are some ideas to generate leads at these events:

1. Note that all of my suggestions above with regard to networking are equally relevant for career fairs. Apply my recommendations about networking at a career fair in the same way that you would apply them at a general networking event.

2. You may consider attending a career fair with a friend, but don't allow the attendance with your friend to limit your options. Your friend's career interests are probably not the same as your career interests. Don't constrain yourself by what your friend likes or does not like.

3. Don't limit your options to only the career fairs at your own college. Other colleges in your area are likely to have career fairs as well, and they probably post the career fair dates on their websites. Most colleges will allow a college student from another university to access their events if the student has proper identification.

Do not limit your attendance at career fairs to only the events taking place at colleges. Many companies and local associations produce career fairs too. Professional societies in your discipline or area of study provide attractive networking opportunities. Throughout the year, association chapters in your area will schedule speakers at meetings as a way of bringing professional members together. These meetings often provide networking contacts for job seekers.

I have not yet discussed some of the most productive sources for networking. These include three sources right on campus that can prove very helpful to you. Your professors often are aware of opportunities. They do not necessarily have jobs in their back pockets to hand out to their students, but they will likely be able to direct you to people who will get you closer to better job contacts.

Another important source of leads and networking opportunities are alumni. There may be events at your college that bring alumni to you. Find out about when these events occur and be sure to attend. Of course, if you are a recent alumnus, you will get an invitation. If you are still a student, you can volunteer to work the registration desk if that is what it takes to get yourself invited to the event.

You can also ask your professors about their alumni contacts. Your professors are more likely to introduce you to alumni than the people at your college charged with alumni relations. This is because the alumni relations staff is usually seeking to raise money from alumni and they do not want to burden alumni with contacts from students seeking a job. Your professors do not have the same concerns, and if they are still in contact with an alum, it will probably be a good contact.

For many students, the largest source of leads will be fellow students. Many students learn about jobs that they do not find of interest. Once they get a job, they often continue to receive leads about opportunities that they will not pursue. If your friends on campus know what kind of a position you are seeking, they will probably be happy to pass on their unused leads to you if the leads match your interest.

To avoid paying a fee to an employment agency, many companies will ask current employees to provide the names of people who might be worth hiring. The companies will often provide a small bonus to their existing employees for referring a prospect that they eventually hire. Friends you made at college may now be working for these companies and your friends may pass on these sources of job leads to you.

You do have one obligation in the process. You too should pass on leads to your fellow students for jobs you have decided not to pursue. Your sharing of leads will not be forgotten. In fact, you may be rewarded in the future for being helpful to others.

Companies where you worked part-time and internships you had while in college are also a source of leads. Even if the job you had was not a professional job, the people you met may have contacts that can help you in your search. If you did a good job while you were there, you can expect that many of your contacts will be more than happy to help you.

Another source of leads is your personal contacts not connected to your profession or school. Your family, friends, and neighbors should not be overlooked. You might think that if they have contacts, they will reach out to you without being asked by you to do so. That is often not the case. Their lives keep them busy and they aren't always focusing on your career goals.

Family and friends may not be comfortable intruding on your job search. They need to be encouraged to get involved. Get them involved by sharing what type of work you are looking for and details about your job search. You may be surprised who manages to find a good contact for you.

It is important that you carefully track all of the contacts that you accumulate during your networking activities. You need to do that so you do not contact any one person too often or neglect to contact someone altogether. Some students use a professional database to keep track of contacts. This is what many professionals do when they use contact management software such as ACT!® or GoldMine.

If you already know how to use one of these software packages, use it to keep track of contacts. You can also create and use a form that you complete each day before closing down your job search efforts for the day. The form below can be used as a format for keeping track of your contacts. You should keep it current and review it periodically to determine when you last had communication with your network of contacts. If you find you are losing touch with someone, consider reaching out to them to build your relationship.

NETWORKING CONTACTS

Name of Contact	Where Contact Was Made	Date Contact Was Made	Organization Affiliation or Occupation	Tel #	E-Mail	Important Info to Remember	Date and Nature of Most Recent Contact

LEVERAGING PRINT MEDIA

An important component of your plan for identifying opportunities consists of the tried and true print media. Many students ignore newspapers because they view papers as "old world thinking." Don't limit your search. Although employment ads in newspapers are declining in terms of frequency, many employers still use newspapers to advertise entry level positions. It doesn't take much time to review newspapers for opportunities. If you are checking on the ads in your local papers and your competition is ignoring the ads, your chances of winning the competition increase.

Beyond newspapers, there is a way to take greater advantage of traditional media that is often overlooked. It represents a unique opportunity for you. Sources of jobs can be found in what we refer to as the "trade press" or "trade publications." Trade publications include the periodicals that cover the activities of a particular industry or profession. Almost every industry sector and profession has at least one and often several publications that report on developments relevant to the industry/profession. Examples include such titles as *Variety* (for the entertainment industry), *PC Week* (for computer industry), *The NonProfit Times* (for charities/foundations/nonprofits), *Chemical Week* (for the chemical industry) and *The Chronicle of Higher Education* (for colleges/universities). These are just a small sample of the relevant set of trade publications available online or through a library.

There are over 10,000 of these publications in the United States and many more are published in other countries. Use of the job ads in these publications represents a unique opportunity. A component of your marketing program to get a job will consist of sending unsolicited letters to prospective employers. Trade publications can lead you to where you can best direct your unsolicited letters to these prospective employers.

There is a challenge to sending an unsolicited letter to a prospective employer. It is often difficult to identify the name or address of the correct person within the company to whom you should send your cover letter/resume – the person who has responsibility for your area of interest. Employment ads in the trade press are often very helpful because many of the job ads in this media include contact information of people that can be the basis for directing your letter.

Most job openings advertised in the trade press are for senior people. The contact people listed in these ads often have responsibility for placing junior or less established people too. In addition, the number of responses to employment ads in trade press media is not often substantial, so your materials are more likely to be noticed and read. Your materials will have a better chance of being forwarded to the appropriate person in the company.

Identifying which trade press titles to search (most of them are now online) is easy. If you don't already know the titles in your area of interest, consult with your professors or local librarians. They will know which trade press titles to use for your search.

If you don't have easy access to a professor or a librarian, you can go on Google and enter the search term "trade publication" and the name of the industry or profession of interest to you in the Google search box. When you do that, more than 100,000 results are likely to appear. For the automotive industry, almost 800,000 results appear. A term as highly specialized as *geology* generates approximately 14,000 results. You can review the first five or six pages of results to assemble enough trade publication titles to get you started on using this valuable source of leads.

Another attractive aspect of trade publications is that they indicate what is going on in the industry – new companies, expansions of existing companies, mergers, and acquisitions.

These industry developments often result in the creation of new jobs. Read carefully and think outside the box about potential opportunities at these companies. You may find some opportunities not yet listed. You could get your foot in the door ahead of your competition.

THE INTERNET

The most popular job lead tool is, by far, the Internet. Using the Internet to get a job has become the major difference in the way people find job leads today compared to 10 or 15 years ago. Students use the Internet more than any other vehicle in their search for employment.

Make extensive use of the Internet. Do not commit the most common mistake when you use it. Do not rely on it as your primary or sole source for identifying opportunities. I see students naively using the Internet and thinking that by doing their five or six clicks a day they have done all that they can do to submit their credentials for a job. This is not the case.

I don't want to mislead you. I love the Internet! I think that Internet job boards can be a rich source of job leads if used effectively. The Internet is the most game changing marketing and technological development in the past 15 years. Much of my teaching and research has centered on the application of the Internet to marketing. However, I have found the Internet can seduce you. It can lull you into thinking that you have covered all the bases in your job search. Do not allow that to happen to you.

In fact, while many jobs are listed on the Internet, most are not. The Internet can be an excellent complement to your search for opportunities. However, you still need to engage in networking to increase your chances of finding employment. This recommendation is supported by expert opinions. Sarah Needleman is a journalist on the staff of *The Wall Street Journal*. In a column *"Experts Weigh in on Job Boards"* in the February 17, 2009 edition of the paper, she reported on interviews she had conducted with experts who specialize in providing career related guidance. Guidance from those experts indicates that networking may be a better use of time compared to Internet job boards and most other tactics.

Students sometimes shy away from the networking related initiatives because it is easier to click on a couple of want ads on an Internet site than it is to go to a networking event. Sorry for the cliché, but what you put into this is what you get out of this. Relying solely on the Internet will diminish your potential to find a job. Include the Internet as a search tool, but don't rely on it as your only method to find a job.

Still, learning how to use the Internet is important to your success. There are some fantastic Internet job sites that you can access and use to find jobs for college graduates. Your Internet job search strategy should include a wide variety of sites.

There are more than 60,000 career related websites. To help you through the process, I have identified a large number of valuable websites that you should access for career information and job listings. Review the list to find what is most relevant for your purposes. Please go to this link to see a summary of these career related websites:

www.thesecrettogettingajobaftercollege.com/careersites.html

The summary not only lists them, but it also describes the mission or objectives of the sites. You can use this information to set priorities for which sites are a good use of your time.

When I instruct students how to use these sites, I tell them to select a few general sites that provide a wide variety of job listings. I also tell them to select a few sites that specialize in the industry or profession that reflects their interest. You should apply this strategy.

Become familiar with the layout of the various sites and their rhythm. By rhythm, I mean the frequency that the site lists new jobs daily or weekly. General sites will list more jobs per day than specialized sites. You should visit both kinds of sites often until you develop a sense of the frequency and quality of new listings. This will help you determine how often to check the sites for new job listings.

In addition to the job site listings and the online version of both trade publications and newspapers, there is another excellent source of job leads. These are the websites of companies and organizations where you would like to work. A recent report noted that to save money on advertising costs, companies are increasing their reliance on help wanted ads on their own websites.

Once you have decided on the geography and industries or professions of interest to you, it is easy to find the companies to investigate with regard to job listings on their own sites. In Chapter Two, I provide you with suggestions how to use market research to find the companies that may be of interest to you.

You can submit your resume for review by the company even if the company doesn't have an appropriate position listed for you. There is a strategy for doing this as well. Chapter Two covers tactics in the development of marketing campaign materials. It addresses how to send unsolicited letters and resumes to companies of interest to you.

EMPLOYMENT AGENCIES

Marketing professionals know that generating leads to build real relationships and produce results requires face-to-face contact. The Internet can contribute to identifying leads, but you still need to put yourself out there. You need to look people in the eye and clicking on websites does not do that. Employment agency contacts are a great way to get in direct personal contact with people who can be of great help to you.

It is important to share with you my views about employment agencies before moving on to the next chapter. Employment agencies are a great source of leads. The people who work at the agencies usually are not paid very much until they place people in jobs. Therefore, they are quite eager to meet new people who they think they can place in a job. They will share qualified candidate resumes with potential employers. I reserved my brief discussion about employment agencies for the end of this chapter because the way you approach employment agencies is very similar to the way you approach a potential employer.

You need to think of employment agencies as representing the employer. They are paid by employers. They aim to please the employers. Many good people work at these agencies and will treat you well. Most will try to help you. However, don't think that they place your interests before their clients, the employers. Their clients' interests always come first. You therefore need to consider all of the tactics discussed in the remaining chapters as equally relevant to employment agencies. Now let's start reviewing the marketing tactics you need to effectively engage employers and employment agencies in your job search.

CHAPTER TWO

Getting the Interview:
Creating Your Marketing Campaign

"Many a small thing has been made large by the
right kind of advertising."
Mark Twain

Only one or two pieces of paper may actually stand in the way of getting the job you want. It is hard to believe that in an age when technology rocks, and bits and bytes seem to drive everything, a piece of paper can make or break your chances of getting your career started. A single piece of paper can be the major obstacle in taking a significant step toward the financial independence you want. Of course, the paper I am referring to is the cover letter or your resume that you send to a potential employer.

Cover letters and resumes need to be treated as part of a package -- your marketing package. Combined with other materials such as a business card and a creative presence on the Internet, these pieces of paper (or electronic files) are probably the most important components of a marketing package to put you in a position to be interviewed. They are important elements of what will propel you ahead of your competition.

MAKING SURE THE COMPETITION IS FAIR

Before discussing each of your marketing package components, it is worth taking the time to understand the tone you need to establish in selling yourself to potential employers. By tone I am referring to how modest or assertive you should be in constructing your marketing package. To appreciate my answer, let's look at the environment you will have to navigate in order to be successful.

Employers' representatives are often excited about their company and believe in what it does. They may believe in its leadership. They may believe in its mission. While the vast majority of employees represent their companies in a balanced way, some, in moments of passionate commitment to their employer, can inflate reality.

To put this in greater perspective, it is worth referring to the work of Jared Sandberg, a well-respected author and journalist. He wrote a column in *The Wall Street Journal* about the truth telling instincts of employers. One particular article, "Short Hours, Big Pay and Other Little Lies From Your Future Boss," which was published in the October 22, 2003 issue, was very revealing.

In that article, Sandberg described what happened to a young man who was promised a job after college at a growing consulting company that advises Fortune 500 companies. The young man was told that he would be solving complex problems and addressing important technology-related issues. He was also promised rapid career advancement, travel, and stock options. What did he actually get? Here is what happened:

"This fairy tale gave way to a scary truth: He spent three months in an empty room in the Seattle suburbs waiting his turn to play BattleZone on the company's fast computer. That was the good part. His longest trip was from Seattle to Portland. He got all of 10 stock options, which

he has since lost. His biggest project was working for the Kings County Jail, where his keenest insight was that the corndogs don't have sticks. He wrote software tracking inmate movement. (How far could they go?) And there was this spooky perk no one warned him about: "The client threatened to keep us there if he didn't get what he wanted."

As that example demonstrates, no organization is always perfectly clear in its communications to job candidates. Select potential employers with attributes closely aligned with your career goals. Some employers highlight only the positive attributes of their organizations. Your challenge is to make certain that you are comfortable with the attributes presented to you and that they fit into your career plan. Always be as thorough as possible in your research about the employer so you have the complete picture of the job opportunity.

Some employers are reluctant to dwell on their organization's shortcomings. Make certain that those shortcomings will not short circuit your career plans. The brief discussion on research in this chapter will aid you in finding out about company problems and other related issues.

To complicate matters, you are competing for the job with a wide variety of people. Not all of these people are likely to have the same sense of moral purpose and honesty that you have. Some of the individuals you will be competing with will actually lie on their resume about their accomplishments. Some of them will more than just stretch the truth. They will bend it to the point where it is no longer recognizable.

Returning to the question of tone, students ask me if they should be completely honest when constructing their resume. The answer is simple. Yes. Tell the truth. Never create fairytales about who you are or what you have accomplished. Lies will often be the undoing of people who are fundamentally honest and qualified. Do not lie in order to level the playing field, but at the same time, throw humility out the window.

Another reason to avoid understating your credentials is that employers will be discounting what you say about yourself. Specifically, many will assume that you are placing your credentials in the best possible light. They assume that some of the candidates will not be entirely truthful. Therefore, some employers tend to diminish the value of what is presented in a cover letter or resume.

If you remain stalwart in not blowing your proverbial horn, you could end up not being heard. If you don't blow your own horn, then who will do it for you? I am not suggesting that you get carried away. Don't exaggerate or appear arrogant. But making sure that you are viewed in the most attractive and appealing way is part of what you need to do in order to get a job. As we review each of the components of your marketing package, keep this firmly in mind!

As discussed in Chapter One, the first step in creating a marketing package is constructing a brand positioning that reflects who and what you are and your desired image. The next step is converting potential employment opportunities into a job. Successful marketing professionals know that the most effective way to convert a prospect into a customer is to understand and demonstrate that you can meet that prospect's needs and wants. Marketing professionals learn about potential customers' needs and wants by conducting market research. You too can use research to convert prospective employment opportunities into job offers.

MARKET RESEARCH

Marketing professionals conduct market research before creating a marketing program. The average person may not be a skilled researcher. Don't worry if research isn't your strength. In the appendix is a simple to follow set of directions to help you conduct your own market research. There you will find some key sources of information that will make your market research quick and easy to do.

Market research is an important component of your overall marketing program. While companies advertising a job opening will list contact information, companies without specific ads present a challenge. For those companies, it may not be readily apparent whom to contact about potential job opportunities. That's when research becomes very important. You need to identify the right person to contact. Your market research will help you to do it.

There is another compelling reason to conduct your own market research. Before becoming a professor, I served as the Executive Vice President in charge of strategy and research for a large public relations agency. Our client at the time was FranklinCovey, which creates and sells personal productivity tools. The company engaged us to create a public relations campaign to announce its merger and new products.

Dr. Stephen R. Covey was a leader of the company. His book *The 7 Habits of Highly Effective People*® provides many principles to help people lead more productive and better lives. One of his most compelling principles is Seek First to Understand Then to Be Understood®. One of the ways you can seek to "understand" your prospective employer is to conduct market research. To communicate effectively with these prospective employers, you need to understand how they work and what influences the way they conduct business. Through your research, you will learn about the influences and business methods of your prospects.

You need to collect and analyze the information relevant to your job search in order to understand the employer and the people you might meet at the company during the interview process. Study the information available, focusing on what is most relevant in terms of understanding the company's aims or business goals, strategies, and culture. Consider the information you gather in terms of how your skills and personality make you a good match for the company and the particular type of position you have in mind.

Remember the discussion in Chapter One. Most college graduates can advance their careers by pursuing a variety of opportunities. They can choose many career directions. You can and you should shape each of your submissions to employers to match what they are seeking in an employee. The best way to create your submission is to understand the potential employer's business, its industry position, and needs. If you know what the potential employer's needs are and what the company is experiencing in the industry, you can write your resume and cover letter to show how you can address the company's needs.

Your market research will give you important information that will help you demonstrate your interest in the company and your ability to serve in a useful role. It will provide you with talking points for your interview. Market research will also uncover information needed to help you decide if you will enjoy working for the particular company.

Conducting the work to understand a potential employer's situation places you ahead of most of your competition. You can obtain much of the information from a company's own website. The areas to examine when conducting a situation analysis include the following:

- Company Overview
    - History of the company
    - Profile of senior leaders

- o   Brands

- o   Key Divisions and Departments

- o   Product(s)/service(s)

- o   Market share

- o   Total industry sales

- o   Sales trends

- o   Geographic locations

- o   Projected growth

- o   Regulatory and government issues

- Profiles of competitors

- Key Trends Impacting the company and its Industry (technological/global/governmental)

- Description of advertising program including key message(s)

You can obtain a substantial amount of information about a company from its annual reports and other publicly available sources discussed in the appendix. Once your research is complete, you will have the information to begin developing your marketing package. Before you move forward, there are other Internet-based research tactics to know to gather more detail on whom to direct your materials at organizations where you want to work.

The first Internet-based tactic I want to share with you is called *Three Degrees of Separation*. Although I gave it its name, a former student first described this technique to me. He brought this

LinkedIn-driven tactic to my attention during his job search by contacting me on LinkedIn. At that time, there was a well-known sports entertainment company where he wanted to work, and he wanted me to introduce him to someone at that company. At first, I thought he was confused because I did not know anyone at that company. I reviewed all of my contacts and could not identify one person at the company. However, that was not the point. Through LinkedIn, many of us know people through other people.

My former student had turned to LinkedIn to reach his desired contact, using a clever LinkedIn feature. This feature allows a member of LinkedIn to search through the database to identify the names of the people who the member's contacts also know. This feature takes the contact finding exercise to another level. It reveals to a member the contacts of the member's contacts and still further, the contacts of that person too.

Returning to the challenge confronting my student, he found out that someone that I knew also knew the person that he wanted to reach out to and seek an introduction. This is why I labeled this process *Three Degrees of Separation*. This takes some time. You need to ask your contact to reach out to his contact and seek his contact's willingness to offer an introduction to someone you want to know. Remember that your contact's contact person probably does not know who you are. So, in my case, I had to first reach out to someone I had not spoken to in more than two years.

Of course, this method may not always work. In the case of my student, it did work. It also can require more time than some people may have patience for. In the case of my former student, it took about four weeks to work through the communications that had to go back and forth between all of the contacts. If you plan well, however, this method can be another way to reach people who are not easily approached. Also, note that this feature was free at the time he used it, but as this book was going to press, there was some discussion that LinkedIn would charge a small monthly fee for this service. If it delivers an invitation to someone at a highly desirable employer's staff, it is probably worth pursuing.

What if you do not know someone who knows the person that you want to reach? What then? The same student who shared the Three Degrees of Separation tactic also invented what he calls *The Job Search Hail Mary*. It is based on a clever use of the Internet and a smart research approach.

Skilled researchers know that we sometimes cannot find all of the information we want located in the same place. They know that sometimes, we have to search in a few places and combine information found in one place with information found in another place. A major challenge in a job search is both identifying the names of the people you want to reach and their respective contact information. That challenge is the central focus of his Job Search Hail Mary.

To identify the names and contact information of the key managers my student wants to contact, he uses information found on a number of different websites. He uses sites such as Monster, Career Builder, Experience, and others to identify the existence of jobs that interests him. He then uses a variety of websites, including Jigsaw, Zoominfo, and LinkedIn to identify names of people and their contact information. Finally, he prepares communications directed to the people he seeks to reach. You will find a description of his process and other social networking tips available on the companion website to this book at the following link:

www.thesecrettogettingajobaftercollege.com/socialnetworking

CREATING YOUR MARKETING PACKAGE

When successful people are asked what contributed to their success, they provide a variety of responses. One particular response I heard many years ago has remained with me. A highly accomplished advertising woman once said that what contributed to her success was that she would "zig when others would zag." In other words, she wouldn't follow the crowd. She would take steps to stand out, to be different.

Your marketing package consists of business cards, cover letters, resumes, and an Internet presence. Let's examine these important marketing tools so you use them to stand out from the crowd.

YOUR BUSINESS CARD

A student with a business card is definitely zigging. This person conveys that he sees himself as a professional. If you think of yourself in this way, others are more likely to see you the same way.

A business card is an essential piece of your personal marketing program. Think of it as a small billboard that not only provides information how to reach you, but also represents you to the people whom you wish to impress. It telegraphs something about you. The color of the card, the font selection (size, type, and color), the size, and type of paper (stock) all make an impression.

Having a business card is not a radical suggestion. It surprises me that more students do not create business cards for themselves. Colleges often encourage it. Trinity College, Utah State, Bates College, American University, and many others recommend that students create business cards. The University of Miami College of Engineering has a program through which it offers students a free box of business cards each academic year.

Many other colleges arrange business card discounts for their students.

Your business card should contain the following basic information:

- name
- landline phone number
- mobile phone number
- mailing address
- e-mail address

Let's review each of these elements. Most people have names that are easy to pronounce. Some last names can present a challenge. What if your first name is also difficult to pronounce? My recommendation is to use an easy to pronounce nickname. If you don't have a nickname, it may be time to create one. The easiest time to do so is when you are starting out on your career path. Don't wait until you are well established to do so.

Please note that some employers (particularly the government) may require your complete legal name in their data systems. If you would benefit by having a nickname, you can choose to do both. You would place your full legal name at the top of your resume. In addition, you would include your nickname at the top of the resume, but you would put it within quotation marks.

I know that the idea of "adding a nickname" is hard for some people. They are proud of their name and its related heritage. You *should* be proud of your name. However, research demonstrates that people with hard to pronounce names may be at a competitive disadvantage. Not everyone may see my suggestion that you create a nickname as politically correct, but it can help remove an obstacle in your effort to get a job.

In Chapter Three, I share some thoughts on telephone numbers and how to avoid telephone-related mistakes. Here, however, I will go over some basics. Choose telephone numbers where you can be easily contacted. If you are planning to move soon or tend to move often, use your cell phone number.

Create a professional sounding, easy to remember email address. Don't use your university email address. You will be graduating and you should assume that someone might still have your business card and seek to reach you after you graduate.

What email address should you use? First, as I already noted, pick something professional. Although you may love a particular movie, comic book character, or activity, choosing an email address that contains "ilovespiderman," "spidermanrocks," or "snowboardingisawesome" is childish and won't make the kind of impression you need to make on potential employers. These email addresses may be fine to use with your friends, but they aren't appropriate in your professional interactions. So, don't use them on your business card, cover letter or resume.

My recommendation is to get an email address with your name as a key part of the address. Do it through a well-known and reliable email service. You can also forward the emails you receive to your "Ilovetorock" or "wildaboutsnowboarding" personal addresses from your more professional address and vice versa.

While you may be zigging while others are zagging, this should always be done in a professional manner. Consider adding a title for yourself on your business card. For example, Bates College provides a sample business card on its website that includes the student's name along with the title of the department reflecting the student's major. The college's sample shows a student's name with the title "Politics and History" beneath it. If you are a student studying engineering, for example, you can list your specialization, "Electrical Engineering" or "Civil Engineering," under your name.

Avoid the title "student" on your business card. Some universities insist upon the title "student" if you use their logo on your card. The problem is that once you graduate these cards will be out of date. Your contact information will change and your status will change too. You will no longer be a student. Additionally, noting that you are a student doesn't add anything. It doesn't demonstrate how you stand out from the crowd.

Your business card provides you with an opportunity to stand out. If you have the space on your card, you can include some other information to differentiate yourself from the competition. Perhaps you have received an award. If so, you can list it on your card indicating, for example, "Acme Award Winner" or "Acme Award Recipient."

I have observed students effectively use a quote of a highly respected professional in their field on their business cards. This can have a major impact if it is carefully chosen. I remember a student who was a Physics major seeking my advice on job prospects. On the back of her card, she had a quote from Albert Einstein. The quote was "Anyone who has never made a mistake has never tried anything new." She indicated that it was often a topic of discussion in her interviews. It was a conversation starter that got her interviews off in a productive direction.

Companies often use taglines in their advertising. It can be a way to remind consumers about what a company stands for and does. I would avoid taglines. Taglines on company business cards are appropriate. Taglines for individuals, however, don't work as well. Personal taglines may come off as pretentious, especially for a recent college graduate. I'm not so sure that taglines work well for highly accomplished professionals either.

You can add useful information on the back of your card. Few people use the back of their business cards and, again, doing so provides an opportunity to be remembered. If you're a language major or if the companies you are contacting have international operations, you can provide a foreign language translation of your contact information. If you're including a quote from a well-established person, the back of the business card could be the best place to put it.

Another consideration in designing your business card is the use of a logo. There are three logo possibilities:

- Use the logo of your college or university - this usually requires the permission of your school.

- Use a logo that you or someone you work with creates for you - this must be done professionally or it can backfire, making you look amateurish.

- Don't use any logo at all - this is the safe route, but can appear bland.

To learn more about creating business cards, you should visit websites that sell business cards. These sites have many helpful hints. In particular, visit www.vistaprint.com and www.staples.com. Both of these sites provide online business card creation services and their prices are quite reasonable.

YOUR COVER LETTER

Who said you can't judge a book by its cover? Many employers rely on the cover letter to make a judgment about how a job candidate presents himself and to get a basic idea of his qualifications. First impressions can be created in a matter of seconds. You can be sure that the cover letter is a major contributor to the first impression that you make. In Chapter Three, I discuss first impressions in great detail, showing how an impression is often created in a split second, impacting how a person perceives and evaluates you.

Treat your cover letter as if it is the most important piece of your package because it just might be exactly that. Clearly, your resume is critical, but your cover letter sets the stage for how your resume will be perceived. Too often, cover letters are written at the last minute by a student who may already have a winning resume and thinks the resume is enough. *A winning resume is not enough.*

The cover letter plays a key role in communicating who you are. It provides you the opportunity to express your personality. Resumes can be shaped to be more than a list of what you are, but primarily follow a pattern that doesn't allow for very much self-expression. Cover letters, done well, can create a high level of interest in people. Of particular importance, a strong cover letter often convinces employers that a job candidate should be interviewed.

As noted in the Introduction, this book is not intended to provide the final word on every aspect of the job search process. Cover letters and resumes are topics explored in many other books. Some of these books are hundreds of pages long. Is it worth the time to read a few of these books? Of course it is. However, these books can be somewhat complicated and provide information beyond the needs of a typical recent college graduate. Most of these books address the needs of people who have been working for several years. So, let me make all of this less complicated.

Your research may identify dozens of cover letter styles and approaches. However, there are really only two basic types of cover letters. The first type of cover letter is a letter in response to a specific job opening that has been advertised. This is referred to as an ad response letter.

The second type of cover letter is one that is sent to an employer when a job candidate seeks a position that may not have been advertised. This type of cover letter is sometimes referred to as a broadcast letter or a cold call letter. This type of cover letter is sent to potential employers in an industry or profession that a job candidate finds of interest.

The two types of cover letters share some common characteristics. They both should be brief. Generally three to four paragraphs are enough to get your point across. Both letters must begin with a first sentence that captures the interest of the reader.

The primary difference between the two types of cover letters is the level of attention each receives. Given the large number of resumes sent to an employer for a particular advertised job, the employer cannot afford the time to read every cover letter. Cover letters in response to a specific advertised job are not usually read as thoroughly as cold call letters. For advertised jobs, the resume is relied upon for most of a job candidate's information. If there is an interest after the review of the resume, the employer will review the cover letter in more detail.

The level of attention given to cold call cover letters is greater, making it a more important component of your package. A large number of resumes are usually not in need of review by the employer. In these instances, the cover letter carries most of the weight to generate interest in a candidate. Your goal in using a cold call cover letter is to persuade the company to find an opening for you or to get you on the top of the list of candidates when an appropriate position becomes available. Your cover letter must be structured so that the prospective employer will be eager to read your accompanying resume.

To get an attention grabbing opening sentence and paragraph requires that you do some research. You need to communicate to the employer that you have done your homework. The employer needs to conclude that you know something about the company or the industry that is relevant to the employer's business.

The research will provide you with information you can weave into the first few sentences of the cover letter and assure other members of the organization that you are worth bringing in for an interview. Here are some examples of brief opening paragraphs that can be shaped and modified for a variety of opportunities:

TO A NEWSPAPER PUBLISHER:

— Your newspaper is increasing its coverage of sports news on the Internet. As an Internet savvy Journalism major reporting on sports events for my university, I believe I can contribute to your news operations.

TO A MEDICAL DEVICE COMPANY:

— It was with great interest that I read about your company's plan to introduce a new hip joint replacement that targets aging athlete and weekend warrior related injuries. As a Marketing major who has already conducted research assessing your market opportunities, I believe I can contribute to your scheduled launch.

TO AN ARCHITECTURAL FIRM:

— The *New York Review of Architecture* reported that your firm expects to retain its number one position in the northeast. I know that my ability and passion for architectural design will make me a valuable addition to your team and contribute to the excellent reputation that your firm has earned.

TO A NONPROFIT FOUNDATION:

— News reports indicate that your organization will be increasing its charitable work to help our senior citizens cope with the tough economy through offering them energy saving services.

My knowledge of energy conservation techniques can contribute to your important work.

TO A RETAILER:

— Your competition in the southwest is increasing its presence in your markets, particularly in Arizona. I can help you maintain and grow your retail business because through my work-study program, I am very familiar with the retail climate in Arizona.

TO A PHARMACEUTICAL COMPANY:

— Scientists indicate your company will lead the way in developing a cure for Alzheimer's disease. I have studied therapies used to treat Alzheimer's disease and I know I can contribute to your good work.

TO A LOCAL BANK:

— The Orlando Sentinel has reported that you are going to place more emphasis on customer service. My experience in working with the public is a perfect match to support your new direction. I have had more than 4 years experience working in customer service related assignments and I am very sensitive to the issues that must be addressed in order to assure a strong customer service program.

Some students don't always have the time to do the research needed to create the strong opening that indicates the circumstances and conditions related to the particular employer. Sometimes a student may not be successful in finding relevant research to support an opening paragraph. In these instances, you still require an attention-grabbing opening.

If you aren't using a research-based opening, focus on a characteristic related to your brand positioning that differentiates you from other competitors for the job you want. My recommendation is to create an opening that speaks to that characteristic. Here are a few examples that are generic in form, but can work (with slight adaptation) for most job candidates and most companies:

— Your company will be facing enormous challenges in the next few years, particularly in terms of increased competition. I would like to contribute my strong set of analytical skills and commitment to your industry to help you overcome the challenges you may face.

— Your company's position in the health care industry will depend upon having employees who are able to help you adapt to the changing industry conditions. My education and industry-related work experiences not only shaped my ability to make the most of a fast changing environment, but also sharpened my skill set to make meaningful contributions within that environment.

Both of these openings share an important characteristic. They sell the candidate's basic skills without any reference to a specific news item. These openings will not be as effective as the research-based examples noted earlier. However, they convey a sharp opening that immediately captures the reader's attention.

Following the strong opening, you need to include more details that describe why you are a great fit for a position. This material would highlight your relevant skills, education, and experiences that are a good fit for the company. This information can be included in one to two paragraphs or in a series of bullets. I prefer using a bulleted format instead of running text. Bullets are much easier to read than text.

Your close should end with some form of "asking for the order." "Asking for the order" is an expression we use in marketing to request some action on the part of the prospect. This is usually in the form of a request for an action to be taken such as a purchase. Close the letter by noting you look forward to receiving a phone call or perhaps that you will call the employer in the near future. You do not want to be too aggressive, but you do want to convey a high level of interest in moving to the next step. Of course, always include your telephone number in the cover letter even if it is already included on the business card that you may have attached to the cover letter.

Now let's put these marketing influenced tactics to work in the creation of a cover letter using an authentic example. Here is an excerpt from a recently advertised job. Some of the details were modified to protect the identity of the employer:

POSITION: ENGINEERING ASSISTANT

Qualifications

- *BS in Engineering or related field*
- *Demonstrated experience in advanced technology*
- *Teaching/ training experience*
- *Good written and oral communications skills*
- *US citizenship*
- *Willing and able to travel locally, nationally, and internationally; must have or be able to obtain a US Passport*
- *Demonstrated customer service background*

The following pages provide examples of two types of cover letters demonstrating maximum impact to obtain an Engineering Assistant position. The first cover letter provides an example of a cover letter that is in response to a job advertisement for the position. To make it more challenging, let's assume that the student responding to this employment ad *did not do the research* necessary to identify and include information relevant to the company's situation. The second cover letter is not for an advertised job. It is from someone who seeks a similar employment opportunity. It is a broadcast letter. Notice that it is not as specific as the first ad response cover letter. This is because there are not specific qualifications already identified in an ad. A broadcast letter is not as aggressive in its close.

Mary M. Smith
11200 Forrestville Avenue
Chicago, IL 60642
312.456.6666
Marymsmith101@yahoo.com

April 22, 2009

Mr. James Lincoln
Stirling Engineering Company
345 State Street
Chicago, Il 06443

Re: Engineering Assistant Position – 4/10/09 Chicago Tribune

Dear Mr. Lincoln:

Your company will be facing enormous challenges in the next few years, particularly in terms of increased competition. I would like to contribute my strong set of analytical skills and commitment to engineering to work with you to overcome these challenges. My skills and qualifications match the opportunity you have available:

- B.S. in Engineering from the Miami College of Engineering

- Demonstrated experience in applying advanced technology to solve engineering problems

- Teaching/training experience in Engineering techniques and practices

- Strong written and oral communications skills

- Born in the United States and have US Citizenship

- Willing and able to travel locally, nationally, and internationally; I have a US Passport

- Demonstrated customer service background in several areas

I am very excited about opportunities that exist at your company. I am eager to begin a discussion with you and so I will call your office next week. I look forward to providing any additional information needed to move our communications to the next step.

Best regards,

Mary Smith

The next cover letter is for a cold call letter or broadcast letter. You should notice a few things about it. These letters are most successful when the job candidate has done research in advance of sending the letter. The opening paragraph must convey to the reader that the candidate has done her homework. The first cover letter to an existing job ad described earlier would also benefit with an opening paragraph that indicates the candidate had done her homework. The cold call letter, however, demands that it be done to grab the attention and interest of the reader.

You will also notice that the list of bulleted credentials is longer in this cold call letter than in the letter to a specific advertised job. It is longer because the candidate will not likely know exactly what credentials will be most appealing to the prospective employer. A recommended approach is to look at advertised jobs at the prospect company or other companies in the industry to develop a list of the most often cited credentials that companies seek for a position in the industry. In doing so, this particular candidate example identified a number of desired qualifications that are often specified in job ads for engineering assistant positions. She then described her background in her cover letter by referencing material, often word for word, that she identified in the engineering assistant job ads.

Mary M. Smith
11200 Forrestville Avenue
Chicago, IL 60642
312.456.6666
Marymsmith101@yahoo.com

April 22, 2009

Mr. James Lincoln
Stirling Engineering Company
345 State Street
Chicago, Il 06443

Dear Mr. Lincoln:

Your company will be facing enormous challenges in the next few years, particularly in terms of increased competition. I noticed that your firm has been competing for major engineering assignments throughout the state of Illinois. In particular, I understand that your next project, the World Towers, will be the largest project your firm has ever undertaken. I would like to contribute my strong set of analytical skills and commitment to engineering to work with you to overcome challenges related to the World Towers project. My skills and qualifications are a very good fit for opportunities at your company. My credentials include:

- B.S. in Engineering from the Miami College of Engineering

- Experience in applying advanced technology to solve engineering problems

- Adept at working with other engineering professionals to develop and train others in the best engineering techniques and practices

- Knowledge of major engineering related software packages

- Excellent oral and written communications skills

- Strong interpersonal skills and collaborative team member

- Great attention to detail

- A self-starter who learns fast

I am very excited about the future of your company. I am equally excited about my ability to contribute to that future. I will call your office next week and I am willing to provide any additional information needed to move our communications to the next step.

Best regards,

Mary Smith

YOUR RESUME

Your resume is a key component of your overall marketing package. A resume provides an opportunity to get your message across to prospective employers, demonstrate your skills and build relationships. It is, in effect, a piece of advertising. It is an ad to help you advance your career.

From this point forward, many of my recommendations treat a resume as an ad. Continue to remind yourself that this is a component of your marketing campaign. You may not have a big budget for newspaper and television advertising. You may not have hired a large professional ad agency to represent you. You may not have hired a well-known celebrity to tell the world to hire you. You are, however, in charge of the most important marketing campaign of your life -- the campaign to place you in the job you want.

I have a few facts that may shock you, but they will help you understand how employers (your target audience) read resumes. These facts definitely shocked me. According to Lisa Parker, a highly respected career coach, the typical resume may only receive 10 seconds of attention from the people reading it. This is not the most shocking part. Here comes the real shocker.

While the typical resume has about 300 to 400 words, people read only about 500 words per minute. This means that in the 10 seconds that the average person spends reading the average resume, only about 25% of a typical resume gets read. The reader will likely ignore the other 75% of the material. In addition, when you think that a few seconds is devoted to reviewing the name at the top of the resume, very little time remains to read the rest of the resume. The conclusion is obvious: there is a high probability only a small amount of the information in your resume will be read.

Think about how much time many people spend working on their resumes. Think about the hours and money people spend trying to construct the perfect resume. Although you may invest a substantial amount of time, many of the people who take the time to look at your resume won't read most of it. Of course, the challenge is even greater since not everyone who receives your resume will even look at it. Allow me to explain why.

The person who will make the hiring decision generally does not do the initial review of a resume. When resumes arrive either by fax, via email, or through the regular mail, they are aggregated and then screened. The person making the hiring decision will not view resumes that don't survive this initial screening.

Resumes are screened primarily in two ways. One way is by junior level employee review. These employees are typically given guidelines as to what is most important in identifying promising job candidates. Most employees doing the screening will make one of two mistakes.

The first mistake is to be too liberal in the review of the initial batch of resumes. In this case, resumes that don't belong in the mix may get sent forward to the hiring manager for further consideration. The other mistake they might make is to screen out resumes that should have gone forward, but are removed from the group of candidates because the employee incorrectly thinks something is missing that should preclude the job candidate from further consideration.

Which mistake do you think the employee is more likely to make? It depends on many factors, including how many resumes are received. My experience has been employees are more concerned about not wasting the time of their "boss" than they are about tossing a deserving candidate's credentials away. If a resume is returned to the employee screening the initial batch of resumes with a note from the boss that it was a waste of time to review, the employee is likely to feel very uncomfortable. Few people delight in receiving negative feedback from their boss about their work, especially when it's avoidable. If a deserving candidate's resume gets tossed, nobody may know that the resume was removed from consideration. Clearly, the junior level employee will likely err on the side of screening out potentially qualified candidates.

These facts influence my recommendations to you. It is obviously very important your resume be viewed as meeting the key job requirements. If there are aspects of your resume that demonstrate that you meet those requirements, it is very important that the information is not buried or surrounded with a lot of irrelevant material. Given the quick and/or partial read your resume is likely to get on its first review, it is crucial that you avoid including many pieces of irrelevant or less relevant material.

There is another reason why focusing only on relevant material is critical. Companies are increasingly using software to screen resumes. It saves them the costs of allocating employee time to conduct the initial review.

The way the software works is as follows. Companies note the keywords that are important to them. Keywords are the words that appeared in the ad for the job. Literally, word for word, the company representatives enter these keywords into the software-screening program.

Most of the resumes received are entered into the same program and the software does the screening. The program scans each resume to identify keyword matches to the job requirements. Each job candidate's resume receives a score that reflects the degree to which the resume meets the job requirements. Those resumes with the highest scores are generally the only resumes that receive further review.

What I have described here also applies to the approach many employment agencies use to screen resumes. Employment agencies often receive hundreds of resumes for a specific job opening and need a way to determine which resumes best match job openings they are responsible for filling. This also includes the resumes accessed from most Internet job boards and social networks.

In constructing your resume, take into consideration these rigid resume-screening processes. Begin by identifying the keywords in job advertisements. Look at the specific ad and analyze it word for word. Review your resume and edit it to reflect the keywords in the job description. Construct your resume (and cover letters) to include those terms specifically. You will get a higher score and increase your chances to make it past the first review.

If you are exploring the existence of a job that is not advertised, the challenge is somewhat greater. However, you can easily overcome this challenge. Find other jobs currently advertised by the employer that relate to your area of interest. Most jobs from a specific unit or division of a company have a similar set of general requirements. By reviewing the other advertised jobs, you will develop a sense of what the employer looks for in job candidates. You can also review job descriptions for the position of interest at competitor companies in the same industry. Identify the words commonly used to describe the job you seek and the required skills. There are common words used in the various industries to outline job requirements. Describing your skills using those words and phrases will increase the chances of your resume progressing through the screening process.

In choosing words to include in your resume that describe what you accomplished, convey an impression you are someone who gets things done. Communicate you are an achiever. Be careful not to repeat words in your description. Many books recommend choosing "power words" or "power verbs" that are strong and descriptive words to include in a resume to describe accomplishments or experiences. The appendix to this book includes a brief list of words you can use to describe accomplishments in your resume. A much more extensive list of power verbs is on the companion website to this book. To view the entire list please visit:

www.thesecrettogettingajobaftercollege.com/powerverbs.html

After assuring yourself that you have incorporated the most relevant keywords in your resume, you have to decide what material to leave in and what to leave out. Let's look at the typical parts of a resume one at a time. In doing so, you will develop an understanding of what should matter most.

THE PARTS OF A RESUME

Marketing is not just about strategy and creative tactics. It's about the nuts and bolts of your work. It's about the details. It's about the look and feel of your resume. Ultimately, it's about the total impact a resume (your ad) makes on its audience. Perception is shaped by how the pieces or details of an image come together. Be sure to pay attention to the details of how you present your image through your resume.

There are some important ways cover letters and resumes can be structured to create an effective look and feel of your materials. Let's review them:

- *Layout and Readability.* Retain as much white space as possible. By doing so, more of the material that matters will be read. Students sometimes cram as much as possible into a resume thinking that it's a word competition. Avoid putting less relevant information in your resume. This will assure you have enough white space to make your resume attractive.

- **_Use of Space._** Be very conscious of how valuable the space is in your resume and use it to its full advantage. Each line of copy is precious. Don't allow one line to extend to a second line if that second line consists of only one or two words. Seek ways to phrase your material to enhance its readability and visual appeal.

- **_Length._** Limit the resume to one page. Even senior professionals usually follow this guideline and they have much to say about what they have accomplished. Again, it's best that you limit how much you expect the reader to review, assuring that they will read more of what you most need them to review.

- **_Spelling and Grammar Errors._** You should do a spelling and grammar check every time you change your resume. Check your resume yourself. In addition, have someone else review it too. Try to find someone with a good eye for detail. Never rely on the grammar and spelling checks that are available with your word processing package. Use them, but don't rely on these programs because they can and do miss details that your eye will notice.

- **_Key Points._** You can highlight key points in a few different ways. For example, provide an extra space between sections of the resume to make each section stand out. Bold or underline important words. Don't bold or underline too many words or your resume will present poorly and look unprofessional. The point in highlighting information is to draw the reader's attention to what is most important. If many things are highlighted, you defeat your purpose.

- **_Emphasis on Results._** If you worked in a function (even as a volunteer or part-timer) in which you produced results, use those results. Share results related to savings, number of customers serviced, number of awards received, and anything that is quantifiable. If you assisted your supervisor in producing the results, you can use phrases such as "Assisted the manager of the store in achieving the highest annual sales for 2009."

- **_Avoid Using Personal Pronouns._** Words like "I," "me" and "my" are acceptable in a cover letter, but these words don't belong in a resume except in a summary statement.

- **_Use Action Words._** These are sometimes referred to as "action words" or "power verbs." These words, as discussed earlier, convey that you are a person who gets things done. Employers prefer people who get things done. Use these words in your resume to convey the sense that you get things done.

- **_Avoid Repetition._** Don't repeatedly use the same action words in your cover letter or resume. Use the list of words included with this book or a thesaurus to find replacement words to avoid repetition.

- **_Use Fonts Consistently._** Select the same font for your resume and cover letter. These two documents often remain attached throughout the interviewing process. Your materials will look more professional when the font selection is consistent.

To help you get started in creating your resume, here's a list of the information typically included in college student resumes:

- Contact Information
- Career Objective

- Summary Statement
- Education
- Honors or Awards
- Experience
- Military
- Skills
- Activities
- Interests
- References

I will provide you with guidance how to address each of the potential sections of a resume so that they are relevant for a college student. Throughout this discussion, remember a recommendation that I made earlier. Don't cram your resume with every detail about who you are and what you've done. Good material is adequate. Great material will win the job competition.

Not all of the sections listed above appear in any one resume. Much depends on the student's characteristics, goals, and the job requirements. Your first task is to assess how much weight to give each of these areas. Weight is the amount of space you allocate to each section in your resume. Allocate the space to demonstrate that you are highly qualified to do the job and that you have the skills to assure you are a great candidate for the job.

You will have to make tradeoffs in the process. For example, if you don't have very much work experience, you will need to give areas not related to work more emphasis. You can add more to the education section of the resume or add more to the activities section. Let's examine each of these major sections of a resume in more depth.

Contact Information

Of course you're going to include this information at the top of the resume. Be certain that your contact information is professional (particularly your email address) and don't rely on your college address. Employers need to be able to contact you after you graduate. Note the discussion earlier in this chapter concerning how best to present a professional email address.

Career Objective

Many people put a career objective immediately below their contact information. I should warn you now my recommendation here is slightly controversial -- although many career services professionals would agree with it. I am not a fan of putting a career objective in a resume and I discourage it in most instances, with good reason.

Typically, career objective statements are vague and add little or no information. They take up valuable space on the resume. Including as a career objective "To work at your company", "Make a contribution in a high growth industry", or "To leverage my skills developed during my education" doesn't provide the employer with much information that it doesn't already know. The employer knows you want a job with the company because you are submitting an application. The employer also knows that most people want to work in high growth industries or leverage their skills. Have you ever heard of anyone stating I want to work in a low growth industry? These types of statements don't set you apart from your competition and you don't need to use them.

As I already noted, space on a resume is very valuable. A typical resume contains about 40 lines of type. Including your career objective will use up 3 or more lines on the page – one or two lines for type, one line above and one below to set it off from the next section. This is not a good use of space.

There is another reason why it's probably best to avoid including a career objective. Every prospective employer has different needs. Address each employer in a customized manner. While a very broad career objective statement can fit almost all employers, it will not add value or distinguish the candidate.

One solution is to create a different career objective statement for each employer. The problem with doing this, however, is that most students do not have the time to change their career objective statement for each employer. Further, if you post your resume on an Internet job site, you can't change the career objective statement so that each employer sees something tailored to its needs. It is best to use the space in your resume for content that will favorably position you to compete for the job you want.

Summary Statement

Professionals with a lengthy work history often incorporate a summary statement in their resume. It usually appears immediately below their contact information. They will use this summary statement as a better way of indicating who they are rather than including a career objective. Using a summary statement can also be a good tactic for a college student.

You should take advantage of opportunities that allow you to reinforce and share your brand positioning with other people. A summary statement affords you the opportunity to feature language that reflects your positioning. It also can be combined with a few other important attributes that you know will be of interest to prospective employers.

By way of example, let's return to the hypothetical Journalism student described in Chapter One. If this student were interested in a job reporting on financial news, she might provide a summary statement such as: "Possess strong writing and analytical skills with substantial attention to detail and a team orientation. Engaged in financial-related study and fieldwork. Conducted financial, investigative reporting and research, worked in financial news-related internship positions."

This summary statement incorporates the student's brand positioning with attributes that employers might find of great interest. Attributes for a reporting job in financial services often include writing skills, analytical rigor, attention to detail, and being a strong team member. By combining material that reflects the brand positioning with job-specific attributes, this summary statement sets the stage for the remainder of the resume. Use of a strong summary statement will likely lead employers to pay more attention to the other sections of the resume.

Education

Your college education has probably occupied most of your time for the past four or five years. Now is the time to highlight it. There are a few guidelines to keep in mind. First, if you attended more than one college, you have a decision to make. Should you provide a listing of the more recent college you have attended or are about to graduate from or should you list all of the schools you have attended?

In most cases, the school that is granting you a degree is the more impressive institution. If that is the case in your situation, you should list the degree granting school. You can augment this by listing a college that you attended through a study abroad program. That provides you with the opportunity to note that you are a global thinker, which is an attractive characteristic in most fields.

Some students list the high school they attended. Generally, I don't think that is a good use of the space on your resume except under exceptional conditions. For example, it would be worth listing your high school if you were the valedictorian of your class or received some other very special honor such as recognition as an all-American athlete. If, while in high school, you attended a pre-college summer program at a prestigious university or college, you can list that experience. In almost all other instances, I would advise against listing high school information. It's no longer relevant. Even if you were the captain of the cheerleading squad or the football team, don't use valuable space to list your high school years.

Grade point average is often a key issue. If you graduated *cum laude, magna cum laude or summa cum laude*, list that honor under education. Many students have a rough first or second year in college. In junior or senior year, they find themselves and blossom. Unfortunately, a grade point average stays with you forever, blossomed and found or not.

If you had a bad first year in college or even a bad first two years, you can list your overall grade point average along with a grade point average that better positions your potential. Here are a few examples:

- 2.9 overall / 3.4 senior year
- 2.9 overall / 3.4 junior and senior years combined
- 2.9 overall / 3.4 in major
- 2.9 overall / 3.4 in Journalism courses

The main idea is not to omit your grade point average. If you do, people may think that it is lower than it actually is. Taking the approach noted in the examples above enables you to demonstrate that you eventually got on the right track in terms of academic achievements. It's a balanced way to present your credentials. You can show your grade point average toward the end of your college career or in your major was better than in your first couple of years at school.

Another tactic is to list the relevant courses you have taken in your college career. Don't limit this list to only the courses in your major. Rather, include courses in other departments that are highly relevant to the career you wish to pursue. Science majors, for example, will want to list statistics and math courses. Journalism majors should consider listing English courses. Government majors should list courses with titles such as Advanced Economics or Intermediate Urban Planning. If you received very good grades in these courses, you can also note the grades for each course.

There is one other very important piece of information that you can add here if it pertains to you. Many students pay for a large portion of their college expenses. They do it through a combination of loans and part-time jobs before and during their college years. Employers respect students who paid their way through college. If you have taken on significant responsibility to pay for college, you should highlight this in the section that describes your education. For example, let's assume that you have arranged for 75% of your college expenses. You should add the phrase "Financed 75% of college tuition and expenses."

Honors or Awards

Honors and awards are often included on a resume. If you have only one or two honors, you should list them under education. However, if you have more than two honors or awards, your collection of honors and awards may merit a separate section on the resume.

You should do more than just list the honor or award by name. Describe it. For example, you can describe it as being selective. Perhaps it is received by fewer than 10% of the student body.

Perhaps it's granted to the student who has exhibited the greatest level of leadership or skill in a subject. Whatever it is for, don't assume that the person reading your resume knows what it is and is impressed by it. You need to highlight and clarify your awards and honors in the resume.

Experience

I often suggest that this section should be renamed "Relevant Experience." The reason is that it allows students to integrate more than just paid work-related experiences. This is of great importance. Most students don't have very much work experience. Any student that does have a lengthy history of relevant experience will stand out from the crowd of others competing for the same job. Using experiences beyond paid work is a great way to achieve a relevant set of *work-related* experiences.

For example, let's look at course work that the typical college student undertakes during the school year. Let's take the case of a Geology major seeking a job related to the environment. If he has conducted a substantive environmental analysis of a specific part of the world in conjunction with a course, he should give it special attention in his resume. Just as a job description could be entered with three or four bullets underneath the job title, this course-related project could be listed in the same manner here. Bullets can be listed under the section on the resume labeled "Geological Environment Analysis Project." A major volunteer effort might be described in the relevant experience section rather than in the activity section if it produced impressive results.

Returning to the topic of paid work such as part-time jobs, these jobs can be described so that the experience gained is viewed favorably. Most students have had a variety of part-time employment. Frequently, they work in retail stores. If a student had responsibility for opening or closing the store (as many do), that is something worth noting. It's also worth featuring responsibilities like training employees, handling customer disputes and accompanying a supervisor on a buying trip (even a local trip).

Many internships are unpaid positions. Often, the intern receives college credit rather than wages. Paid or unpaid, the features discussed with regard to part-time jobs apply here as well. Frequently, an internship will include a variety of professional-related aspects. The intern might be asked to accompany a supervisor on a sales call, analyze data, or generate ideas to improve operations. These are not clerical functions. These are professional experiences and should be featured within this section as well.

As you describe your experiences, list them in reverse chronological order. The most recent experience should appear first in this section followed by the next most recent experience and so on. Don't worry if some timeframes overlap. It's common for internships, relevant part-time jobs, and college projects to occur at the same time.

You do not need to list every job, internship, or project you have ever done. People who have been in the workforce for many years have to account for their time and avoid gaps. They are expected to list all of their employment experiences. That doesn't apply to a college student or recent college graduate.

In Chapter Four, I will share with you what you should do if you haven't found a job several months after graduation. As for college students and recent graduates, don't list jobs or experiences that are not relevant to your field of interest. In this way, more attention is placed on the experiences that are relevant.

As you go back in time, you don't need to provide as much detail about the experience unless it is highly advantageous to do so. Jobs you held in your first or second year of college may have only two or three descriptive bullets. Jobs that you held in senior year will likely have additional descriptive bullets.

Military

Increasingly, people who have served in the military return to school to obtain further education. If you have a military background, you should include a description of it in your resume. Military experience is highly regarded by most people. People with military experience are able to follow orders, give orders and work as collaborative team members. They are viewed as disciplined and as having a tough exterior. Therefore, if you've served in the military, include a description of that experience in your resume.

The jobs you held and training you received in the military may be relevant to the jobs you are seeking now. Identify the relevant military jobs and training and list them as attributes under the section that describes your military experience. Spend time on your own or with a career counselor to translate your military experience into the appropriate job functions that you now seek in civilian life. This will help you achieve a good match between military and civilian occupations.

Do not use jargon-laced abbreviations that only people in the military will understand. Always include in the description of your military experience a listing of certifications and licenses you obtained while in the service. If you received any form of a security clearance, be sure to include that in your resume. It will impress people who read it.

Skills

This is the section where you should describe the hands-on skills relevant to the type of position you're seeking. Computer-related skills, including software proficiencies, should be listed here. List them only if the programs are relevant to doing the job you are seeking.

If you don't have many computer-related skills, but if you do know how to use a word processing package or are good at searching the Internet, then you can list those skills. If your skill set is much greater than Internet searching and the use of word processing programs, omit the Internet searching and word processing skills since most students would be expected to possess these skills. The goal is to list skills that show that you are qualified and have greater skills than your competition.

In addition to computer-related skills, list other technical skills here. Health-related professions, for example, might require knowledge of CPR or training in other medical techniques and equipment. Fluency in a foreign language is another example of a skill you could note in the skills section of your resume. Many students have earned certificates or licenses that document a proficiency in a career-related skill. Certificates and licenses would be listed here.

Activities

This section of the resume is where you share what you did outside of the classroom. Emphasis should be on community or college related extracurricular projects. Almost everyone respects people who volunteer. It demonstrates an attitude of sharing and being unselfish toward others. In organizational life, you might be called upon to act in an unselfish way. Here is your opportunity to show that you have already done so.

Club, council and team memberships could be listed in this section. Note, however, that your resume will be more effective if you go beyond listing activities. You should indicate what you did or accomplished. For example, if you volunteered in a soup kitchen, what did you accomplish? Did you feed more than 250 people each weekend for a year? Did you provide assistance for more than 100 families in a homeless shelter?

If you worked at a club, were you an officer? Even if you didn't serve as an officer, were you in charge of an important initiative? Perhaps you were responsible for a club membership drive, financial management, or event programming. Perhaps you grew the membership by 40% or you implemented a strategy that resulted in a 30% cost savings. Providing details about your activities is important. It's better to list a few activities and provide more details about what was accomplished at each one than to list several activities without detailing what you accomplished.

Choose the activities that are most congruent with the job you want to obtain. You may have a long list of clubs, teams, and volunteer organizations you have supported. Only include the activities that reinforce your credentials for the preferred job. For example, if you're seeking a job in the health care profession, noting you volunteered at a local nursing home is more important than referencing your work on the school yearbook. If you're planning to enter the financial services industry, your role as the treasurer of the student council is more important than your involvement in other non-financial activities.

Interests

In the interests section of your resume, you have the opportunity to insert your personality and indicate what aspects of life turn you on. People prefer to work with those they find interesting or with whom they share a common interest. Successful sales professionals know that people want to do business with people like themselves.

You should list interests that are likely to generate a common bond or, at the very least, get the conversation going so that a common bond can be formed. Be very selective about what you include. For example, noting that you enjoy reading may not get you very far. Everybody reads. Enjoying it is not distinctive enough. Better topics are an active participation in a sport or travel to specific areas of the world (as opposed to travel in general). Another topic would be hobbies that require a lot of skill (chess) or perseverance (mountain climbing) and anything related to music (particularly if you play a musical instrument).

Stay away from politics, religion, and any other potentially controversial topic. Material related to these topics may win you a friend, but they could generate resistance from members of the interviewing team. Not everyone on the interviewing team likely shares the same religious or political views.

References

Many resumes contain the statement "References available upon request." Every time I see that statement, I cringe. It's a waste of space. Similar to the earlier discussion regarding the career objective statement, providing a section like this removes lines of space that could be better used to your benefit. Do some students actually think that employers don't know that a candidate will provide a reference or two if they ask for it? Of course, employers know that and so, such a statement should be omitted.

While a general statement that "References are available on request" is a waste of space, if the student knows someone who is very prominent in their field of interest, it may be worth putting that person's name on the resume within a references section. Make sure to get permission from the person you intend to list as a reference before adding his or her name to your resume or reference list. Don't put the person's contact information in the resume. Instead, provide it if requested to do so and be certain that the person will respond quickly to a reference request.

Chapter Four will provide more details concerning the handling of references.

The following pages provide sample resumes. You should review these resumes and apply aspects of them that relate closely to your situation – your major and your job interests. Before you review the resumes, however, you need to understand the rationale behind my formatting decisions.

When considering the entire array of resume formats that are possible, it can be very confusing. There are literally thousands of different possible resume formats. Choosing the appropriate one can be quite daunting. There are so many variables.

For example, just considering font size (10-, 11- or 12-point) and font type provides dozens of possibilities. Deciding whether to use text or bullets presents more possibilities. Putting headings to the left of a resume section or at the top of a section presents further possibilities. You also need to decide whether to indent, double indent or not to indent at all. Additionally, you need to decide whether to use a paragraph format or bullets.

I once had a student who asked me for my opinion about her resume. She came to our meeting with more than 80 versions. She spent more time on the formats and layout than she did on creating the important content!

To spare you all the time that she devoted to format, I have provided a sample resume for popular majors on the following pages. Along with these samples, I provide the following warning:

Each resume should reflect a combination of the job candidate's credentials (including major), the type of job he is seeking and the needs of the prospective employer. You can't take a sample resume, simply change a few items, contact information, and assume you are ready to go with it.

Two English majors applying for the same job at the same company will, and probably should, approach the resume development process differently to reflect their individual credentials. The same job title at two different companies (with different requirements) will likely require job candidates with different types of skills and resumes.

I have selected a format that I consider optimal in providing good use of space. It quickly communicates the important aspects of a candidate's credentials. I used Arial font in 11-point or 12-point type. Arial looks better on a computer screen than many other fonts. I used section heads placed on the left and bulleted text rather than paragraph text.

Use the following sample resumes as a starting point. *Don't apply these samples blindly to your situation.* You'll have to use your judgment in developing your own resume after applying the principles previously discussed in this chapter.

The first three resume examples that appear on the following pages are in this order:

1. English major seeking a communications position with no military experience
2. English major seeking a communications position with military experience
3. Business major seeking a retail trainee position

These examples reflect many of the principles discussed earlier in this chapter. The first two resumes are for people who have the same objective and similar experiences with one exception. One student was in the military. The resume belonging to "Nancy" reflects her military experience. In order to include this additional relevant material, Nancy needed to use a smaller font size (11-point font rather than 12-point font). Material included in these resumes was selected to obtain a communications related position.

The third resume is for a Business major. This student is interested in retailing and uses his retail positions to emphasize that he is comfortable interacting with the public, something that an entry level retail professional will need to do on the job. The resume for "Richard" describes a person who may have also worked on the yearbook just like Mary and Nancy, but that credential is not included in his resume. It is not included because it is not very relevant to the position in retailing that he is seeking. He may share the same interests such as playing the piano and soccer, but his volunteering at a soup kitchen is more relevant. Retailers prefer employees to be involved in the local community and Richard's volunteering delivers on this objective.

English majors and Business majors are two of the more popular majors on college campuses. These examples provide you with guidance in constructing your resume even if you are not an English or Business major. If you would like to see a resume relevant to your major, then I strongly encourage you to send an email to:

info@thesecrettogettingajobaftercollege.com

You should describe your major in the email. I will create sample resumes for other majors in response to receiving these emails. You will find these examples posted on the following web page:

www.thesecrettogettingajobaftercollege.com/resumes.html

> **Example:** English major seeking a communications position with
> no military experience

Mary English Major
999 E. 84th Street, New York, NY 10075 ● mary10001@aol.com ● 917-xxx-xxxx

---

English major with excellent research, writing and editing skills and experience. Thorough attention to detail and an effective creative approach to assure an engaging and informative communications style.

EDUCATION: **National University,** New York, NY
Bachelor of Arts, English, May 2009
GPA: 3.46 overall/3.68 in major, Cum Laude
Coursework: Professional Editing, Non-Fiction Writing, Poetry, Writing in the Disciplines, Field Reporting, Ethics in Reporting
Project/Honors Thesis: Conducted research and authored 30 page report analyzing the role of immigrants in business innovation

EXPERIENCE: **Public Relations Assistant/Intern**, September 2008 - Present
Armani Exchange, Kingston, NY
- Assisted Communications Director developing and executing strategy resulting in broad media coverage of product launch
- Developed brochures and other collateral material
- Represented company at industry events

Writing Center Tutor, January 2006 - August 2008
National University Writing Center, New York, NY
- Counseled 150 students concerning term papers
- Directed changes resulting in high quality report writing

Sales Associate, June 2005 - December 2005
Abercrombie & Fitch, Orange, NY
- Provided customer sales support
- Handled daily cash and opened and closed the store

ACTIVITIES: **STUDENT GOVERNMENT,** September 2007 - Present
- Provided publicity for all club events
- Developed 30% increase in student participation

YEARBOOK, September 2006 - May 2008
- Decreased production costs by 15%
- Maintained relationships with collegiate and local vendors

SKILLS: **COMPUTER:** Word, PowerPoint, Publisher
LANGUAGE: Fluent in Spanish

INTERESTS: Photography, Piano, Soccer, Poetry

> **Example:** English major seeking a communications position with military experience

Nancy English Major
999 E. 84th Street, New York, NY 10075 ● nancy20001@yahoo.com ● 917-xxx-xxxx

English major with excellent research, writing and editing skills and experience. Thorough attention to detail and an effective creative approach to assure an engaging and informative communications style.

EDUCATION:
National University, New York, NY
Bachelor of Arts, English, May 2009
GPA: 3.46 overall/3.68 in major, Cum Laude
Coursework: Professional Editing, Non-Fiction Writing, Poetry,
    Writing in the Disciplines, Field Reporting, Ethics in Reporting
Project/Honors Thesis: Conducted research and authored 30 page
    report analyzing the role of immigrants in business innovation

EXPERIENCE:
Public Relations Assistant/Intern, September 2008 - Present
Armani Exchange, Kingston, NY
- Assisted Communications Director developing and executing strategy resulting in broad media coverage of product launch
- Developed brochures and other collateral material
- Represented company at industry events

Writing Center Tutor, January 2006 - August 2008
- National University Writing Center, New York, NY
- Counseled 150 students concerning term papers
- Directed changes resulting in high quality report writing

Sales Associate, June 2005 - December 2005
- Abercrombie & Fitch, Orange, NY
- Provided customer sales support
- Handled daily cash and opened and closed the store

MILITARY:
Communications Specialist, June 2002 - June 2005
U.S. Army, 101st Airborne Division, Fort Campbell KY and Iraq
- Managed information distribution of command decisions
- Liaison to 18 post and community newspapers

ACTIVITIES:
STUDENT GOVERNMENT, September 2007 - Present
- Provided publicity for all club events
- Developed 30% increase in student participation

YEARBOOK, September 2006 - May 2008
- Decreased production costs by 15%
- Maintained relationships with collegiate and local vendors

SKILLS:
COMPUTER: Word, PowerPoint, Publisher
LANGUAGE: Fluent in Spanish

INTERESTS:
Photography, Piano, Soccer, Poetry

Example: Business major seeking a position in retail

Richard Business Major
999 E. 84th Street, New York, NY 10075 ● richard30001@gmail.com ● 917-xxx-xxxx

Business major with excellent leadership skills and experience working with demanding customers in a public or retail setting.

EDUCATION: **National University,** New York, NY
Bachelor of Science, Business Administration, May 2009
GPA: 3.46 overall/3.75 in business courses, Cum Laude
Coursework: Management ● Marketing ● Statistics ● Leadership ● Financial Management ● Operations Management ● Economics ● Retail Management ● Sales Management
Project/Honors Thesis: Conducted research and authored 30 page report on the future of Internet retailing

EXPERIENCE: **Retail Intern,** September 2008 - Present
- Armani Exchange, Kingston, NY
- Assisted sportswear buyer in developing and executing strategy resulting in the launch of new line of clothing
- Contributed to the planning of purchases for the 2009 season
- Represented company with vendors to plan inventory

Retail Clerk, January 2006 - August 2008
- National University Book Store, New York, NY
- Counseled students concerning textbook selection
- Supported development of merchandise sales tactics
- Executed inventory restocking program

Sales Associate, June 2005 - December 2005
- Abercrombie & Fitch, Orange, NY
- Provided customer sales support
- Handled daily cash and opened and closed the store

MILITARY: **Communications Specialist,** June 2002 - June 2005
U.S. Army, 101st Airborne Division, Fort Campbell KY and Iraq
- Managed information distribution of command decisions
- Resolved hundreds of complaints or inquiries among community groups concerning post activities

ACTIVITIES: **STUDENT GOVERNMENT,** September 2007 - Present
- Obtained 15 sponsorships with local retailers
- Developed 30% increase in student participation

SKILLS: Word, Excel, PowerPoint, Access

INTERESTS: Travel, Volunteer at New Covenant House Soup Kitchen

---

Example: Education major seeking a position as a teacher

Michael Education Major
999 E. 84th St., New York, NY 10075 ● mike30001@gmail.com ● 917-xxx-xxxx

---

Education major with substantial teaching experience in an inner city environment. Combine a love of children with significant preparation in applying innovative and tested techniques to achieve desired learning outcomes and student development.

EDUCATION: **National University,** New York, NY
Bachelor of Education,   May 2009
Concentration in Elementary Education
GPA: 3.25 overall/3.45 in Education courses
Certification: State of New York Elementary Education; CPR

TEACHING EXPERIENCE: **Student Teacher**, September 2008 - Present
New York City Public School System, Brooklyn, NY
- Instructed 45 second-grade students in all priority academic areas
- Assisted in more than 100 parent/teacher meetings
- Responsible for classroom management
- Successfully integrated science into the reading program

RELATED EXPERIENCE: **Librarian for Children's Literature**, January 2006 - August 2009
Brooklyn Public Library, Brooklyn, NY
- Assisted teachers in local schools in finding age relevant literature
- Provided assistance in creating content to be used in library brochures and website, highlighting literacy and library collection
- Created interactive forum among children to share favorite stories

Swimming Instructor, June 2006 - September 2008
YMCA, Kingston, NY
- Supervised children ages 5-14
- Instructed children in life saving techniques
- Trained children ages 10-14 in competitive swimming

HONORS: Dean's List for 6 semesters, Kappa Delta Pi International Honor Society in Education, Brooklyn Special Recognition Student Teacher Award

ACTIVITIES:
- National University Yearbook: Associate Editor
- National University Volley Ball Team: Team Captain

INTERESTS: Piano, Mountain Climbing, Volunteer at Brooklyn Science Museum

---

Example: **Engineering major seeking a job in designing electrical components**

Susan Engineering Major
999 E. 84th St., New York, NY 10075 ● susan30001@gmail.com ● 917-xxx-xxxx

---

Engineering major with experience solving complex engineering and design problems. Excellent analytical skills combined with knowledge of relevant computer software programs and ability to work with teams to address challenging projects.

EDUCATION:	**National University,** New York, NY Bachelor of Science, Electrical Engineering, May 2009 GPA: 3.25 overall/3.45 in Engineering courses

Coursework:
Digital Signal Processing ● Multivariate Statistics ● Advanced Digital Circuit Design ● Project Management● Solid State Devices ● Engineering Seminar

Independent Research: Integration of Digital Circuits in Environmental Systems. Report presented to IEEE Conference

EXPERIENCE: **Engineering Intern,** September 2008 - Present
Sumitomo Systems, Kingston, NY
- Provided assistance to Engineering Manager in assessing applications for scheduled sub-systems; delivered report 30 days ahead of schedule
- Contributed to division engineering plan for 2009
- Represented company at software symposium

Retail Clerk, January 2006 - August 2008
Adco Electrical Supply House, New York, NY
- Worked with contractors in identifying relevant electrical supplies
- Supported development of in store merchandise displays

SKILLS: Feedback and Control Systems, Signal Processing, Wireless Communications, Firmware Coding, Matlab, C++, MS-DOS

ACTIVITIES: **Society of Women Engineers,**   September 2007 - Present
- Programming Chair, arranged for presentations over a two academic years by 10 different industry professionals addressing a variety of Important engineering developments
- Provided outreach to local community building projects

INTERESTS: Mountain Climbing, Volunteer at New Covenant House Soup Kitchen

---

Kathleen Nursing Major

999 E. 84th St., New York, NY 10075 ● kathleen10001@aol.com ● 917-xxx-xxxx

---

Nursing major with strong clinical training experiences, including several certifications and licenses. Very importantly. adapt easily to changes in environment and scheduling while maintaining a positive attitude and concern for patient care.

EDUCATION: **National University,** New York, NY
Bachelor of Science in Nursing May 2010
GPA: 3.36 overall/3.6 in nursing and health related courses
Clinical Experience: Practicum consisted of more than 200 hours at the Veterans Administration Hospital. Assisted with care of patients recovering from amputations, post traumatic stress syndrome, spinal cord injuries and arm, leg and knee replacements.

EXPERIENCE: **Wellness Center Assistant**, September 2008 - Present
Kings County Senior Center, Brooklyn,, NY
- Assisted in the care of 450+ senior citizens
- Administered medication and related compliance
- Provided training in the use of medical equipment

Health Education Instructor, June 2007 – August 2008
YMCA Summer Camp, Brooklyn, NY
- Taught CPR to high school students
- Assisted in health education lectures

LICENCES & CERTIFICATIONS:
- New York State Registered Professional Nurse License #9999999, expiration July 2012
- BLS, ACLS, PALS Certifications, May 2009
- EKG Certification, May 2009
- Diversity Training certificate, May 2009
- CPR, April 2006
- Catheter and IV training, July 2008

HONORS:
- Student of the Month, October 2009
- Sigma Theta Tau

SKILLS: **COMPUTER:** Word, PowerPoint, Publisher
LANGUAGE: Fluent in Spanish

INTERESTS: Volunteer at the Brooklyn Homeless Shelter, Piano, Soccer

---

Example: Nutrition major seeking a job in a community health organization

---

Katherine Nutrition Major
999 E. 84th, New York, NY 10075 ● katherine30001@gmail.com ● 917-xxx-xxxx

---

Nutrition and Dietetics major with substantial field experience and a passion for healthy eating. Experiences include both designing nutrition programs and providing instruction to children and adults concerning healthy diets and lifestyles.

EDUCATION: **National University,** New York, NY
Bachelor of Science,   May 2010
Nutrition and Dietetics
GPA: 3.2 overall/3.55 in Junior and Senior years

FIELD
EXPERIENCE: **Clinical Rotation**, September 2009 - Present
Gunderson Hospital, White Plains, NY
- Assessed health concerns of 80 patients
- Identified etiology of concerns
- Developed nutrition care plan for patients

Community Rotation, September 2008 –August 2009
Millwood Community Center, Peekskill, NY
- Contributed to the Millwood mission to improve the health of center members and promoted healthy lifestyle changes
- Participated in more than 100 counseling sessions
- Created, implemented and led community outreach programs

RELATED
EXPERIENCE: **Medical Records Clerk**, January 2008 - August 2009
Yonkers Medical Center, Yonkers, NY
- Assisted patients in retrieving medical records
- Processed 30 to 40 insurance claims on a daily basis

Swimming Instructor, June 2007 - September 2007
YMCA, Kingston, NY
- Supervised children ages 5-14
- Instructed children in life saving techniques

HONORS: Dean's List for 5 semesters
Kappa Omicron Nu Honors Society, Chapter Event Coordinator
Employee of the Month, Kingston YMCA

ACTIVITIES:
- American Dietetic Association, student member
- National University Volley Ball Team: Team Captain
- Volunteer, Meals on Wheels

INTERESTS: Piano, Mountain Biking, French Cooking

Example: Biology major seeking a job addressing the environment

---

Robert Biology Major
999 E. 84th, New York, NY 10075 ● robert30001@gmail.com ● 917-xxx-xxxx

---

Marine biology has been the primary focus of work throughout college career. Substantial experience in assessing environmental hazards both in the field and in college labs and have a strong knowledge of the relationship between chemical and biological conditions.

EDUCATION: **National University,** New York, NY
                         Bachelor of Science,   May 2010
                         Biology
                         GPA: 3.2 overall/3.4 in science courses

                         Related coursework: Plant Biology ● Human Genetics ● Marine
                         Mammalogy ● Marine Microbiology ● Evolution ● Statistical ● Chemistry I
                         and II ● Biological and Chemical Interactions ● Introduction to Ecology

                         Senior Term Paper: Conducted research and analysis on environmental
                         changes to Connecticut shoreline and the effects throughout the Long
                         Island Sound. Based on this research, published a working paper with
                         professor and delivered presentation to science faculty.

RELEVANT
EXPERIENCE:

                         Water Testing Assistant/Internship, September 2008 –August 2009
                         Westchester Water Engineering, White Plains, NY
                         • Recorded data from meters, recorders and other sampling devices
                         • Submitted samples to laboratory for testing
                         • Assisted in development of report preparation and recommendations
                           for more than 100 inspections for 20 miles of coastline

                         Marine Camp Instructor, June 2007 - September 2007
                         Seacamp, Big Pine Key, FL
                         • Develop instructional materials for high school students in ecology
                           and the role of marine sciences
                         • Instructed more than 300 campers over 30 sessions in on
                           developments and future prospects of marine science
                         • Led fields trips to undeveloped islands and assesses soil samples

ACTIVITIES:
                         • Science Club, Chair of speakers bureau, arranged for 10 lectures
                           from experts on the nature of the environment
                         • Student Newspaper, Reporter on science fiction movie reviews
                         • Volunteer, Hammonasset State Park, assisted in obtaining financial
                           support for the marine biology lab for children

INTERESTS: Tropical Fish Collection, Scuba Diving, Soccer

r

Example: Political Science major seeking a job in government

Mimi Political Science Major
999 E. 84th, New York, NY 10075 ● mimi30001@gmail.com ● 917-xxx-xxxx

Government has always been my passion and engaging all members of the community to participate in the process is my goal. It has shaped all of my work experiences. I have had substantial experience in analyzing legislative and governing issues at the federal, state and local levels and bring experience in working with voters and leaders in and out of government.

EDUCATION: **National University,** New York, NY
Bachelor of Science,   May 2010
Political Science
GPA: 3.2 overall, Dean's List
Related coursework: Comparative Politics, Community Engagement ●
International Politics ● Public Policy ● Political Polling ● Parties and
Elections ● Statistical Analysis ● Economics I and II ● Community Finance
Senior Term Paper: Conducted research and analysis to assess best
practices in improving community involvement in the electoral process,
resulting in a 40 page paper and a poster presentation to student assembly

**RELEVANT
EXPERIENCE:**

Legislative Assistant/Internship, September 2008 –August 2009
Office of State Senator Harvey Smith, Peekskill, NY
- Development of email newsletter to more than 100,000 constituents informing them of the Senator Smith's committee activities
- Participated in more than 50 community outreach sessions
- Assisted in the creation and implementation of 10 programs to inform the community about benefit eligibility under the new federal laws

Membership Associate, June 2007 - September 2007
YMCA, Kingston, NY
- Trained teenagers to supervise younger students as camp counselors and team leaders
- Liaison to parents to assure their children had positive experiences, conducted 50 parent meetings to resolve questions or concerns

ACTIVITIES:
- College Yearbook, Club Vice President in charge of sales, increased yearbook sales over the previous year by 25%
- Student Council, Chairman of Student Engagement, increased membership in student clubs by 15% over the previous year
- Volunteer, League of Women Voters, New Rochelle chapter

INTERESTS: Guitar, Scuba Diving, Soccer

Your Internet Presence

One of the most exciting marketing developments is the Internet. The Internet allows people throughout the world to "meet" each other, exchange ideas, and share interests. It's a channel for candidates and employers to become better acquainted.

Chapter One provides information about using the Internet to find information about an opportunity or to send your resume to a company. You can use the Internet for more than that. You can use it as a tool to share more information about yourself than will fit in a resume and to place your credentials where prospective employers can find you and contact you about a job.

Chapter One also discusses the power of a strong personal brand. The Internet provides terrific tools to make your personal brand rise above the crowd, stand for something that you believe in, and represent how you want to present yourself to other people. If you have not used the Internet to bring attention to your professional side, now is the time to do so. You can expect that, over time, having a professional presence on the Internet will become the norm. For now, it will set you apart from your competition.

My recommendation is to start with something simple. If you aren't on a social networking site, you should immediately sign up for one. It shows that you're not adverse to technology; that you're serious about your job hunt; and that you are willing and able to network, all of which are important to the majority of companies or organizations. Most of the popular social networking sites such as LinkedIn and Facebook are available free or for a small fee if you subscribe to a premium version. In addition to using these sites to stay in contact with people, you can post longer versions of your resume and include links to other relevant materials to highlight your skills and accomplishments.

However you choose to present yourself on a social networking site, I strongly recommend that you separate your personal life from your professional life. Here is what I have observed about the material posted by some of my former students and my friends on Facebook. My experience viewing their materials provides a lesson how to manage your public image and your brand. I usually "friend" my students after they graduate. Their photos can be entertaining and provide a window into each one's personality. Occasionally, I share a post or message with them. It's an easy way for us to stay in contact no matter where we move or live.

Sharing aspects of your personality or a photo of yourself with your new significant other is certainly acceptable among friends. Pictured chugging a bottle of your favorite beverage may get comments from your friends. Many friends may give your photo a "thumbs up" and post replies about how funny the photo is and how happy you appear in it.

But ask yourself: Is this photo one you would ever attach to your resume or portfolio to share with a prospective employer? My recommendation is to maintain a professional social networking image. While you can share personal aspects of your life, do so with caution. There is a possibility that people other than your friends may be viewing your material. You should assume that a prospective employer is viewing what you have posted. Some recent news stories provide a sense of how your "privacy" may not be so private.

On October 18, 2010, news stories appeared across the United States about Facebook. Apparently, one or more of the applications found on Facebook had the potential to reveal information about the identities of its users on Facebook. A few days later, it was reported that MySpace had been sharing with its advertisers data that can be used to identify profiles of its users.

Never forget that for Facebook and MySpace to survive financially, they both need to cooperate with advertisers. As advertisers and application developers learn more about people on these sites as well as the sites of other social networking communities, it is likely that more private information will be leaked to companies. Some of the leaking may be accidental. Some of the leaking may be intentional. Therefore, you have to assume that the information can work its way into the hands of people in charge of employment decisions.

Maintaining separate personal and professional images on different social networking sites will not completely prevent others viewing your posted materials. Employers may check you out on the popular sites. It only takes a few minutes to do so. You can't blame them for wanting to know more about you. They need to know if they are going to be working with a "normal" person or a psychopath with dangerous obsessions.

You need to take steps to protect your brand and your reputation given these developments. The following are a few suggestions to control what people learn about you. To provide additional privacy protection, some students use a nickname in registering and securing a page on a social network. They share their nickname with only the people they trust. Then they use their full names for a different account for professional identification. Having two accounts is something to consider if the materials you post are not universally politically correct.

Many pieces of information on social networking sites may remain accessible in one way or another. So even when you don't share your social networking pages with your prospective employer, take a fresh look at those pages. Purge them of any photos or information you think will detract from your image if an employer were able to access the material. Check your security settings to confirm that people other than your friends cannot access information which you prefer to keep private. After you have made any changes to your security settings, test them to determine if you were successful in making the adjustments.

Twitter is another outlet you can use to provide the world with your point of view about the things that matter to you. If you tweet, review what you have already posted on that site. Be sure the material is appropriate for an employer to read. If you aren't sure about the acceptability of your material, you should remove it.

Twitter limits the length of your tweets to 140 characters. It is difficult to be constantly glib and brilliant with that limitation. If you have read tweets, you know that a substantial amount of the material is rarely brilliant and in fact, most material is rather unremarkable. Many tweets are not worth the brief time to read or they do not pertain to professional goals. My conclusion about Twitter: Unless you are constantly spewing fabulous truths about the world around you, use the functions on Twitter to keep your tweets private and expose your tweets to only your friends.

Up to this point, I have been guiding you about what not to do with your social media pages. I do not want you to become part of the crowd that may potentially become embarrassed by postings on a site. Yet, you can make the Internet and its tactics work harder for you in the development and execution of your marketing program. There are steps you can take to do this.

First, search yourself on all major search engines, such as Google to identify information about you that appears in the results. A thorough search helps you see what a potential employer can uncover about you on the Internet. This step is particularly important because before candidates are asked to participate in an interview, many employers will search their names on the Internet to learn more about the candidates.

Employers are interested in learning things a candidate has accomplished as well as any less than attractive elements that a company would prefer to avoid seeing in a job candidate. As discussed, if you have material online that you are not proud of, you usually will be able to remove it. If you cannot remove it, take steps to push the unwanted search results down so that they do not appear at the top of the first page of results. Posting more positive material about yourself on other sites may help push the unwanted search results down on a page.

Create a profile on LinkedIn to ensure you have an Internet image that a) you control and that b) you make consistent with your personal brand. LinkedIn brings unique benefits to your job search. One of my marketing consulting colleagues is Lonny Strum, founder of the Strum Consulting Group. Lonny has contributed to some of the most successful marketing campaigns in the United States. He has identified several key benefits of LinkedIn through his review of what top executives and other leaders are doing with the LinkedIn service. These two benefits rise above all others:

- Reconnecting with people you know, but may have lost touch with. Lonny notes that it can be awkward to call someone out of the blue after many years of not having had any contact. However, it is much less awkward to contact someone via LinkedIn. The renewed contact may then lead to speaking and broadening a relationship. As noted throughout this book, relationships are the foundation of building a career and job opportunities.

- Joining groups that are relevant to your background and interests. By doing so, you come into contact with people who may represent new professional relationships and maybe even potential new friends. You will learn much by following the conversations within the groups.

To leverage the power of LinkedIn, be certain that your presence provides the world with the best view of you and where you want to go. Following more advice that originates from Lonny, here are a few tips to remember that are especially relevant to recent college graduates:

1. Post a professional photo. Do not use your Facebook photo from your high school graduation or for that matter, from any graduation unless it is professional.

2. Fill out your profile with everything that matters. Include all jobs, all collegiate experiences, groups, associations, honors, awards, boards, and highlights of your time at school.

3. List all past employers, not just recent ones, because providing a list of the more distant employers is the best way to connect with more people who may remember what a great job you did in your part-time job or internship. These contacts can lead to renewed relationships.

4. Join as many groups as possible. Lonny states that some people have joined 50 groups! He believes more is better, and I believe he is correct. He notes that you don't have to show all of the groups on your profile. Yet, a larger universe of contacts will become available to you if you do join many groups.

5. Update your status often to keep others updated on what you're doing. Updating gives people an opportunity to think about you each time they see your name and learn of something new that you are doing.

Chapter One also mentions blogging to support your networking opportunities. If you establish a blog, it will likely appear near the top of the first page of a set of search engine results if someone searches on your name. Thus, blogging is a way for employers to find you. If you hold strong opinions on matters related to your career interests, a blog can be a strong tool. Developing a blog is easy. Similar to social networking sites, there are many free blogging sites. These sites can have you up and blogging in a matter of minutes. Blogging doesn't have to be a daily activity. The important points are to *not* be too controversial and to be sure that your grammar, punctuation, and spelling are correct.

If you are not the best writer, ask someone you trust to edit your blogs before you post them. Have others check your content for readability before you post. Read your blog aloud to yourself before you post to make sure you haven't inadvertently left out a word, easy to do when you don't type well!

After you have accumulated several blog entries, you then can consider linking the blog to your social networking site and listing the link to your blog in your resume. Further, you can use your blog material to submit the material in the form of an article to an Ezine. Ezines are the Internet's version of a magazine. Typically, Ezines have an industry focus or topic that they specialize in that attracts web visitors with similar interests. The articles are short. By submitting an article to an Ezine for publication, your name is more likely to appear higher in the results section of the search engines when someone searches your name. Most importantly, your article will appear in connection with something consistent with your professional goals.

A step up from both blogging and social networking is creating your own website. You can use your website to post all your social networking and blog content in one place. Your own website provides you with the opportunity to shape your profile. You can include all types of information in addition to your blog or Ezine articles. You can post your resume with links to pictures of yourself receiving awards; your letters of recommendation; and your best school projects. You can provide photos taken on trips around the world to demonstrate your global perspective, something important in today's economy.

Again, a variety of free to low-cost website services exist that can have you up and running in less than a day. If you're not facile with HTML, don't be concerned. Some easy-to-use solutions involve less time and money than what designing and coding your own website might require.

In addition, an important development has emerged on college campuses over the past five years: ePortfolios. Many colleges are providing ePorfolios to their students and faculty because these personal pages have the look and feel of a website. These sites help to mark the academic progress of students. They provide a wonderful tool to store and archive your work so that prospective employers or graduate schools can view your accomplishments. Using an ePorfolio, you can store photos, videos, term papers, drawings, paintings, articles, letters to an editor, science projects, PowerPoint slides, letters of recommendation, and just about anything else that you think will present your personal brand in the best possible manner.

Prior to the creation of ePortfolio software, many students created similar pages on the web with services provided by Internet companies, such as Yahoo! or Google. However, ePortfolios provided by colleges have an important advantage over the services offered by commercial companies. First, even after you graduate, you can make changes to your college provided ePortfolio because access to your ePortfolio stays with you forever in most cases. In contrast, commercial companies can and will merge, sell, change their focus, or otherwise stop your service. Yet it's unlikely that your college will not continue to operate.

Second and just as re important, most colleges modify the software so that you can limit who sees what. As a result, not all of your work is visible to everyone. You can choose on a case-by-case basis what each prospective employer needs to see. This attribute is not often available on commercial web pages. As a side benefit, if someone wants to friend you on Facebook, you can use your ePortfolio as a substitute, avoiding insult to anyone whom you do not want to have as a "friend" on Facebook.

Because there are so many ways to create an ePorfolio, I have created a page on the companion website to this book with links to a variety of student ePortfolios in different disciplines. Please go to this link to review some of the examples along with brief commentary as to what I like about each one:

www.thesecrettogettingajobaftercollege.com/personalbrand

Whether you create your own website or an ePorfolio, all of your Internet-accessed content can be linked together. Blogs, social networking sites, and your own website/ePortfolio should be viewed as an interconnected web of material that reinforces who you are and what you are about. As you create a web presence, be sure to keep the focus on your brand positioning. Your content should be consistent with the way you are positioning yourself so that you are always presenting an image that fits with your brand positioning and career objectives.

YOUR PHYSICAL MATERIALS

Although many of your submissions will be done electronically, you will most certainly send letters and resumes the traditional way as well -- through the United States Postal Service. Pay close attention to the stationery you select for your resume and cover letter. It should be high quality and at least 28 lb paper. You can go as high as 32 lb paper at a slightly higher cost.

Avoid being too "colorful" in your paper selection. Fancy colors may make it look as if you are trying too hard. In addition, employers sometimes fax resumes to other members of a company and colored paper does not always look good when it is faxed. The best colors to use are white, off-white or ivory. They are crisp, clear, and provide good contrast. Many employers prefer white, but off-white and ivory work well too. Avoid use of all other colors.

If you have a budget for it, your envelope should match the color and quality of the paper you place inside it. In addition, you might consider arranging to have your return address printed on the envelope. Match font styles and graphics in all of these materials. You should not be using different fonts for the envelope, cover letter, and resume.

Type the name and address of the addressee unless you have great penmanship. Always make certain you have affixed the correct amount of postage. A postage due notice from the post office to your prospective employer will not score points. Even if you have access to it, do not use a business postage meter to apply the postage. Use of postage meters appears too commercial.

Although people have the opportunity to create custom postage stamps today, don't try to make a statement with the stamp. Use plain and simple postage stamps. You can make a statement in other, better ways.

At times, it is appropriate to include some component of your student portfolio along with your resume and cover letter. There are times when a sample of your work may impress the employer. If the employer in a job ad requests a writing sample or other material, pay attention to the instructions and be sure to send along what has been requested.

If you are sending an unsolicited letter, including a sample of your work might help you break through and get the recipient's attention. You must, however, be absolutely certain that the sample of your work will be understood and well presented. Great work, taken out of context, can often be received poorly. If you decide to include a sample of your work, take the time to include a description with it that explains what it was for and why it was effective.

UNSOLICITED APPLICATIONS

Many of your applications will be in response to an advertised job. However, most job openings are not advertised. The companies you might pursue for opportunities may not have an advertised position. You can conduct market research to identify companies of interest and the appropriate people to contact at these companies.

In sending unsolicited applications, try to identify at least two people as points of contact to receive your materials at each company. Be sure to list all the people you contact on the letter you send. In effect, you are making each person aware that the other person also received your inquiry. This accomplishes a few objectives.

The individuals will now have an opportunity to consult with each other to decide which one should take your inquiry and move it forward or inform you that there is nothing at the company for you. Given that they know that others received your inquiry, they are not as likely to totally ignore it and throw your letter in the circular file (known as "the garbage can").

Sending your materials to more than one individual and copying them also avoids an embarrassing situation. There have been instances when job candidates have directed their inquiries to many people at the same company without letting each person know that others at their company were contacted as well. If more than one person becomes interested in the candidate, it will be a problem for the candidate at some point. Eventually, there is a very high probability that all will find out about the multiple contacts and this will present an internal company problem. People begin to think that the job candidate is playing them off each other and that usually ends up as a problem for the job candidate.

YOUR MARKETING PARTNER: HOW TO WORK WITH CAREER SERVICES

You will receive advice from a wide variety of people as you plan your job search. Most people offer assistance out of concern for your future. Parents, friends, and professors will likely have much to say about what you should do and how you should do it. While the advice may come at you from all corners of your life, pay closest attention to the input you receive from a career services counselor at your school. Career services counselors are professionals dedicated to understanding the employment environment.

When you have built a relationship with a career specialist over the course of your academic career, he or she will know a lot about you. If you have not yet developed a relationship with one, start now. It is never too late to start. The counselors focus on matching students with opportunities that maximize students' potential to move in the best career direction. Their advice should be weighted most heavily. Think of the people you meet in the career services department as being your *marketing partner* in the development and launch of your campaign. You will see that is exactly what they can be and much more!

Your career services counselor is your quality control guru. You should not expect your counselor to do all the work for you because you are in charge of your campaign. You have to put in the time and effort into creating your success. If you schedule visits with your counselor at the right time in your job search, your counselor will contribute substantial value to your effort to find a job. Guidance from your counselor can improve the quality of your job search and your chances for success.

In my research for this book, I spoke with leaders in career services organizations throughout the United States. My question to all of them was the same: "What is the best way for students or recent graduates to get the greatest benefit in their work with a career services unit at a college or university?" I found many offered similar advice, and I want to share their best advice with you.

First, begin as early as possible in working with career services. Starting early provides you with the time you need to work through all of the steps discussed in Chapter One. Steps such as identifying the vision for yourself, defining your brand, and using these important elements to craft your elevator speech set the stage for your marketing package. The career services staff can assist you in moving forward with this work, especially if you already have been building a relationship. It also gives them time to reflect and suggest valuable adjustments to your job search efforts.

Second, attend the workshops and orientations provided by career services. Note that some schools require you to do so, or they will limit access to their services. They want students to be well prepared to increase the chances for successful outcomes by their students. In addition, career services organizations have a strong interest in their students doing well in interactions with employers.

Career services staff have an interest in protecting the reputations of their school and the students they send out to the world of work. They know that when a student sends a poorly prepared cover letter and resume to an employer, the employer will not be as interested in receiving resumes from other deserving students at that school. They know that when a student does not perform well in an interview, the employer may not be as interested in interviewing other students from their school. For all these reasons and because they are dedicated people, they want to help you so that you perform well.

Third, be sure to check the website of your career services unit because these usually offer helpful materials to accelerate your progress. You may find tips on resume preparation, how to interview and much more. You may find job openings, including those that are exclusive for students attending your school. Many times, alumni who want to give back to their school by hiring someone from their school post jobs through the school's career services unit. You will want to check the website often as new jobs are posted weekly or even daily.

Next, be an advocate for yourself. Remember that the ratio of students and alumni who have access to a career services unit can result in more than 500 people seeking assistance per counselor, depending on the size of your school. Counselors are busy people who constantly juggle the needs of many students, alumni and employers at the same time. Seek ways to stand out; yet remember to be gentle in your advocacy of your need for assistance. It is good to be assertive. It is just as important to remain polite.

Job seekers need to stay top of the mind with their career counselor. Check in every month to remind your counselor you are still looking for a job so they keep you in mind when opportunities surface at the companies and organizations they contact.

Further, come prepared to your counseling sessions. Bring a list of questions and your final drafts of cover letters and resumes.

Show the counselor your materials and ask for his or her opinion. Inform your counselor what you said on an interview and ask for feedback about whether or not what you said is appropriate. Do not, however, expect your counselor to create your cover letters and resume for you. Those tasks are your responsibility.

Do not become defensive when your counselor provides critical feedback. Do not make your counselor feel as if you do not want to hear what they have to say. Remember they may have 499 other job candidates who are listening with an open mind and willing to apply the counselor's advice to get a job.

Finally, and very importantly, notify your counselor when you have obtained a job. They too need feedback about how well their efforts are working. Your getting a job is an indicator that their work is on target. Career services counselors do the work they do because they enjoy it and they want to know the results of their efforts on behalf of their students.

Getting a job can take significant time, and in this economy, it takes longer than it used to. Demonstrate patience in your relationship with career services personnel. Some people get lucky and obtain a job almost immediately after they begin their search. For most people, it takes time. In working with career services counselors, do not allow any impatience you may have to affect your relationship with your counselor. Your counselor is as eager to see you receive a job offer as you are.

Thank your counselor and everyone in the office that helped you obtain a job. While it may be their job to help you, they deserve a thank you each time you seek their help. Once you begin your job, a big thank you is in order.

Do not forget to give back to your school and the career services organization. Provide them with your contact information at your place of employment. When you learn of a job that becomes available at your new employer, inform your career services counselor, and try to put your counselor in touch with your employer.

Last, in the new economy, your first job probably will not be your final job. Take time to come back to your school if possible to mentor the next generation of graduates. It is not just a good thing to do. You will develop a reputation as a supportive member of the alumni and that too is a reputation building opportunity for you. Importantly, your career services contacts will appreciate your support.

We have been fortunate to receive reviews and helpful suggestions from many members of NACE and other career professionals. We have summarized their suggestions and posted the material on the companion website to this book. Please go to this link to review this additional valuable material:

www.thesecrettogettingajobaftercollege.com/careerservices

THE VALUE OF PERSISTENCE

Chapter Three provides tactics borrowed from successful salespeople and interviewees. Applying these tactics will help you sell yourself as you begin to generate leads. If you follow the recommendations I have shared with you, job leads will convert to telephone calls seeking an interview with you.

Remember my description that you are engaged in a numbers game. You need to generate as many leads as possible in order to find potential job openings that result in the launching of your career. It will take work, but the work will pay off if you are persistent. I am reminded of a plaque that my grandfather had on the wall in his office. It had a quote attributed to President Coolidge about the value of persistence. It is worth a moment of reflection:

"Nothing in this world can take the place of persistence. Talent will not; nothing is more common than unsuccessful people with talent. Genius will not; unrewarded genius is almost a proverb. Education will not; the world is full of educated derelicts. Persistence and determination alone are omnipotent."

If you remain persistent and follow many of the recommendations in this chapter, you will find yourself interviewed for a job you want! Now, let's prepare for that interview.

CHAPTER THREE

Acing the Interview:
Building a Relationship and Selling Yourself

"Never wear a backward baseball cap to an interview
unless applying for the job of umpire"
Dan Zevin

In marketing, we often refer to identifying and getting customers as a "numbers game." To generate a large number of prospects, you will need to work hard at your marketing campaign. The more leads we generate, the more likely that one or more of the leads will turn into a sale. The more leads you generate in your job search, the more likely that one of those leads will turn into an interview that provides you an opportunity to sell yourself.

The initial contact from an employer will often come in the form of an email. However, many employers also choose to initiate contact with a phone call. This is your opportunity to start building a relationship. Marketers refer to this contact as a "touchpoint." A "touchpoint" represents a moment in time and a relationship building opportunity in which you can greatly influence how the prospective employer perceives you. Let's look at these moments of opportunity.

INTERVIEW: SELLING YOURSELF OVER THE PHONE

Increasingly, the first formal interview is conducted over the phone. It may be conducted by an employment agency or with the company that has posted a job opening. These interviews screen out candidates whose face-to-face interview would be a waste of time.

Your first task is to remove any background music you may have embedded or linked to your voice message on your telephone. Many students have recorded music either as a prelude to a voice message or as background enhancement. It may be rock, rap, or some romantic riff on a saxophone. Although it is all good (I am a big music lover), you need to get rid of the music during your job search. Most employers view music linked to your voice mail as unprofessional.

Your voice message should be simple and to the point. A simple, but appropriate message could be "You have reached Mary Smith and I am not available at the moment, but please leave a detailed message including the purpose of your call and I will return the call as soon as possible." You do not need any more information than that.

Always return the call within a few hours of receiving it. Employers tell me that a large percentage of students take more than a day, and some take up to a week, to return a phone call. In the competition for jobs, a slow response time to a prospective employer almost guarantees your elimination as a potential employee. Excuses such as "My cell phone battery died" might work with a friend or some college professors, but it will not usually be accepted by a prospective employer.

Always have a pen or pencil and a writing pad with you when you are on a job search so that you can take notes during a phone call. Document the information given to you by the caller (job description, etc). Also record your responses to each of the questions you are asked.

After an initial job phone contact, I often ask students about the details of the would-be job. Many shrug their shoulders and indicate that they forgot to ask! Although much of the conversation will be in the form of the caller asking you the questions to determine your eligibility for the job, you should also be prepared to initiate questions. Here are some reasonable questions you should consider asking at this first contact:

- *What are the job responsibilities?*
- *To whom would I report?*
- *Is this a new job or is it replacing an existing one?*
- *If you are informed that this position replaces an existing one then ask: What happened to the person who had the job you are now looking to fill?*
- *What is the targeted start date?*
- *Whom am I going to be meeting with during the interviews? Be sure to get correct spelling of names and the titles of the people you will be meeting with so that you can conduct research about their backgrounds.*
- *How did you find me? This feedback lets you know whether a particular Internet job board or networking activity is working for you or if the contact was in response to a cold call letter or an advertisement.*

Answers to these questions will help you when you move further along in the job interviewing process. Notice the absence of some questions that should not be asked at this time. Questions such as "How much does it pay" or "What are the benefits" are best not asked at this time. The caller probably will have reviewed your resume and has a sense of your experience. The compensation will usually be in the right neighborhood as a starting point for negotiations. Later in this chapter, I have a few suggestions if the interviewer asks you about your salary objectives. For a detailed discussion on salary negotiations, please review Chapter Four and its discussion on closing the sale.

Be sure to find a quiet place to return the phone call so you can hear the other person. If you are in a very noisy area and you receive a call from a prospective employer, ask if you can return the call in a few minutes so you can find a quiet area. The person on the other end of the phone will always understand the need to do that. If an appointment is made for a return call, be sure to keep it. An employer waiting by the phone for your call that is never received is not something that will serve you well.

In establishing an appointment for an interview, obtain all the contact information about the employer. At a minimum, get the employer's phone number and email address. On the day before the appointment, confirm it. Have the employer's information available so if you have an emergency on the day of the interview, you can reschedule it.

Try not to schedule more than one appointment per day and allocate enough time for the interview. If the employer likes you, the interview may last much longer than you had anticipated, so do not schedule anything too soon after your interview. You should do everything you can do to avoid rescheduling an appointment, but life (and particularly public transportation) can alter our schedules. It is best to notify an employer immediately if you know there is a problem keeping an appointment.

Preparing For the Face-to-Face Interview

Prior to conducting a sales call, successful salespersons seek as much information as possible about the company and the people they will be calling on to make a sales pitch. As a prospective employee, you need to do the same thing. Long before you arrive for the interview, you should have completed your general research on the employer and its industry. Chapter Two provided you with tips on research related tactics. Now you need to conduct more detailed research on the company in order to identify the issues relevant to your interview.

You should have identified the names and the titles of the people you expect to meet. Some of the people may have given speeches or written articles on topics that you can read before the meeting. They may be tweeting on Twitter and if so, you will learn more about them and their point of view. Through your research, you may gain insight about the people you will meet in the course of your interviews.

For example, you may identify the college they attended, a sport that they have played, or a community board that they serve on in your area. You may find that you (or a close family member) share interests or experiences that may be referred to during your interview. The more you can find interests or connections that you share with the people you meet, the greater the possibility of developing a bond with them.

Bring your business cards with you and provide a business card to each person you meet. Ask for the business card of each person you meet. This exchange can be done at the very beginning or the very end of the interview, but it is important to do it. If a person you meet does not have a business card with them, be sure to get the correct spelling of their name and their contact information at the end of your conversation with them.

You will likely meet more than one person during the course of an interview. Many companies are well organized and arrange for everyone you meet to have reviewed your resume before they meet you in person. However, not all companies are well organized and not all people who may interview you are well organized. To keep everyone informed about you, bring extra copies of your resume to the interview. This will demonstrate that you are well organized even if the employer is not.

Print your resume on attractive high quality paper. Bringing copies of your resume on attractive high quality paper provides you with yet another opportunity to distinguish yourself from other people seeking the same job that you want. Differentiating a brand was discussed in Chapter Two and you need to look for every opportunity to differentiate your brand. Before we examine the questions you might be asked, here is one final comment about preparation for the interview – be sure to turn off your cell phone. Interviewers find it very annoying when a cell phone rings during an interview so shut it down and put it away for the interview.

THE INTERVIEW: SELLING YOURSELF IN PERSON

As you wait to be greeted by the people you expect to meet, use this time to put yourself in a better position for the interview. Do not make any phone calls while you are waiting. Instead, use this opportunity to notice the surroundings of the workplace. You might even start a conversation with a receptionist in the area.

Arrive about 15 minutes early so you will have the time to better prepare yourself for the interview. Use this time to review your notes about the job. You should also use the rest room to be sure your hair is neat and that your wardrobe meets your objectives (nothing unbuttoned, untied, or untucked). A planned early arrival also provides a cushion for any delay in transportation arrangements.

Most importantly, arriving early provides one of the most important advantages for a candidate. It allows the candidate the opportunity to observe the people going in and out of the workplace where the interview is to take place. That can be helpful in developing a sense of the corporate culture of the workplace. Examine the physical space/facilities of the company. There may be a magazine or company report in the waiting area that provides information about the company. There may be pictures, photos, or awards on the walls. Look at the way people greet each other. Pay attention to any notices posted on bulletin boards.

These materials may provide insight about the organization. You may also find a way to work your awareness of such material into one of the interviews as a way of noting you are insightful and what happens in the workplace matters to you. Observing and reflecting upon what you have observed provides you with material to jumpstart the conversations that you are about to have with the employees of the company.

It is particularly important to be respectful of the receptionist and any other people you meet who may not be senior people, but whose opinion of you could matter and might influence how you are assessed by the hiring organization. It is not unusual for hiring managers to ask receptionists what they think of individuals who are brought in to be interviewed. Never assume that the less senior people do not matter because their opinions may influence hiring decisions.

The interview may take place in a manager's office or in a conference room. It may be conducted with one person at a time or with several people. Regardless, always greet each person mindful of the impression that you are making. Pay attention to your body language. Throughout the process, maintain good posture and do not slouch when seated. You do not have to stand at attention like a soldier on guard duty, but avoid appearing too casual and relaxed.

START OF THE INTERVIEW

At the beginning of each interview, ask if it is permissible to take notes. It would be unusual for any hiring manager to say no, but it is always appreciated when someone asks permission to do so. It also calls attention to how thorough you are by taking notes. Of course, if you do ask, be sure to actually take notes. Focus on the key facts that you will likely refer back to later in the interview or on another day at a subsequent interview.

One of the important principles in marketing is that it is the goal of every management team to bond their brand to their consumers. We seek to create a connection between the brand and the target audience. The same thing is true in seeking a job. During the interviewing process, you have a great opportunity to create a bond with the people interviewing you. Find a connection with them. Seek the common ground that can be the basis of a relationship. The interviewer is probably wondering, "Do I want to work with this person and spend time with this person?" You want the answer to be "Yes."

You are also screening the employer. You too should be asking yourself if you want to work with the people you are meeting. Do you want to spend 40 to sometimes as many as 60 hours per week with the people who are interviewing you? Do you want to spend time over a cup of coffee or late nights in a conference room working on a project with them? If the answer is "No", then maybe it is not the job for you. The interviewing process is a way to find the answer.

Where you are interviewed may provide an opportunity to build the bond you seek with the interviewer. If you are interviewed in a manager's office, this is another opportunity to pay close attention to the surroundings or trappings of the office. Are there trophies for a particular sport on the bookshelf? What are the titles of the books and have you read any of them? Is there a photo, diploma, or certificate on the wall? These are all potential cues to identify and make a more personal connection with the interviewer. For example, if you notice a trophy for a sport that you play, it is easy to refer to it in the conversation and indicate how you too enjoy the sport.

Many interviews are with more than one person at a time. In these circumstances, it is important that you make as much eye contact with all of the people interviewing you. Inexperienced job candidates will often make the mistake of spending most of their time looking in the direction of one person. That one person might be the highest-ranking person or the most attractive person. No matter who it is, it would be a mistake to spend all of your time looking in one person's direction. You do not need to set your watch to determine how much time you spend in eye contact with each person. Your eye contact does not have to be that precise. It is important, however, to move your gaze in the direction of everyone. In that way, nobody will feel slighted.

We have an expression in the advertising business that is shared by many of us who develop marketing campaigns. It is that "We never get a second chance to make a first impression." It is very difficult to undo the initial impression that someone has formed of you. Once someone thinks you are this or that, your impression will probably remain for the duration of your interaction with them. You need to manage the presentation of yourself at each step of your interaction with the people who interview you.

How quickly are first impressions formed? Research suggests it may occur in just a few seconds. In his best seller *Blink*, the author Malcolm Gladwell noted that in a matter of a few seconds, interviewers already have an idea of which job candidate they will hire and which they will not hire.

Gladwell's book has been a popular success, but science may have proven him wrong. Researchers at Princeton University conducted experiments using photos of people and asked the people in the experiments to rate the people in the photos based solely on the photos. The people were rated on traits that included attractiveness, competence, trustworthiness, likeability, and aggressiveness. Their research indicated that many people form judgments about other people in a matter of one tenth of a second!

Consistent with making a good first impression, you need to be attentive how you look to others. Do not worry if you do not look like a famous movie star. In fact, if you look at the leaders in America, very few look like Brad Pitt or Angelina Jolie. You just need to look and act professional. However, starting with your personal appearance, it is a good idea during the interviewing process to look in the mirror before each interview. This is a time to be attentive to personal grooming habits. You might usually be well groomed, but this is a time to be somewhat more obsessed about it.

Unless you are going to work in a very creative field such as the art, film, or music business, you should avoid purple or green streaked hair and metal on or in your ears, nose, or eyebrows. Women can certainly wear earrings, but that is probably the entire amount of metal or precious gems one should expose to interviewers. If you have a tattoo, even if it is endearing and has the words "Mom" embedded in it, you will be wise to cover it up now. Be sure your clothing covers the tattoo in its entirety.

How you dress matters. You can make one of two errors. First, you can be underdressed. On the other hand, you can also be overdressed. I always advise candidates to visit the potential work location in advance to observe the mode of dress. You can consult with people who know someone that works at the company to develop a sense of the style of dress at the company. There will be occasions when these tactics are not always possible. Therefore, my general advice is to arrive slightly overdressed. For men that means a tie and a suit or sport jacket. For women that means a skirt and blouse and closed toed shoes.

When planning your wardrobe, try to avoid expensive labels. Armani clothes are great if you can afford them, but leave them at home. If you wear them, the interviewer may think you do not need the job. Except for a watch (and earrings for women – as long as the earrings are not large and dangling), you can leave the rest of your jewelry collection at home too. When you get the job, you can consider wearing all of that, but not for the interview.

As you are greeted by the receptionist or the interviewers, keep remembering the total first impression you wish to leave with your prospective employer. Having good posture, a strong handshake, and good eye contact will set the tone and establish you as a confident self-assured person. Employers do not hire people who they think are weak or insecure, so let them know you are not one of those weak or insecure people.

There have been so many good books written about body language and I encourage you to read one. There is one important aspect of body language we need to examine in more detail. I want to address the handshake.

The handshake is critical. Research has indicated that people are more likely to remember you if you shake their hand. A survey reported by human resource professionals indicates they are likely to remember an ineffective handshake more than tattoos or body piercings. We cannot over emphasize the importance of the handshake.

It is said that men are better at handshakes than women. The reason could be that men get more practice as teens shaking the hands of others in connection with sports. This may or may not be true, but everyone needs to be sure his or her handshake is a strong one.

The art of a good handshake is one of the areas that surprisingly, many college students need to master. Many college students have weak handshakes. A few things to avoid: do not hold the other person's hand longer than a few seconds or a few pumps of the hand. If you are someone who suffers from cold, clammy hands, then be sure to wipe them moments before you know you are about to shake someone's hand. I know that this may sound over the top, but be sure your hands are dry.

When shaking someone's hand, provide the entire hand and not just a few fingers. Unless you are the Queen of England and are expecting your hand to be kissed, provide all of your fingers and expect to grip the other person's hand in its entirety. While shaking hands, maintain direct eye contact. You will be maintaining eye contact throughout the interviewing process and the shaking of hands is no exception.

When someone tells you their name during the handshake, as a way of remembering their name later, repeat it immediately before you say your name. For example, if they say, "Hello, I am Mike Jones" then say, "Hello Mike, I am Mary Smith, great to meet you." As an aside, most people like to hear their name mentioned and so repeating the person's name out loud, not only helps you to remember them, but they will be more likely to remember you too.

As already noted, many good books are available that include discussions how to dress and how to leverage effective body language. I encourage you to read a few of these books. The Internet also has substantial material in the form of videos you can review for helpful hints on these topics. I have identified relevant videos and provide a link to them on the companion website to this book. Please go to this link to review the videos and in some cases, my commentary about them:

www.thesecrettogettingajobaftercollege.com/interviewappearance

THE INTERVIEW: YOUR SALES PRESENTATION

Answers to the questions you will be asked during the interview provide you with an opportunity to sell yourself. Think of it as a sales presentation. Each question provides you with an opportunity to make a sale with your answer.

The people you encounter will be doing more than just assessing your technical skills. They will form opinions of you as to what kind of a person you are and do they want to work with you. They will be asking themselves if they like you. Liking you will go a long way to contributing to the decision to hire you. The interview provides you with a great opportunity to tell your personal story in a way that allows the people you meet to like you.

I have reviewed the many and varied questions that are asked during telephone and face-to-face interviews. The total number of potential questions can number in the hundreds. There are however, 40 questions that probably account for the most often asked questions. Think about your answers to these questions before you start the interviewing process.

Actually, think about these questions the moment you apply for a job. If the telephone rings and someone on the other end of the phone begins to ask you one of these questions, what will be your answer? To help you through the process I have listed the 40 questions below. I have taken it a step further. In most cases, I am going beyond listing the potential questions. I am also providing you with the rationale behind the questions so you develop a better appreciation of the employer's objective when asking a question. In most cases, I also provide some potential acceptable or unacceptable answers.

Here comes my warning and a reminder. I cannot emphasize this enough:

The range of answers that I provide are shared with you so that you develop a sense of what is and what is not acceptable. Every person is different. Every employment opportunity is unique. What works for one person for one job may not work for someone else. Develop your own responses to these questions and do not simply replay the responses that I am providing to you.

You are the best judge of what you are capable of delivering in terms of answers to questions. You need to read these questions and answers to develop your own internal compass that generates the best answer for you. The best answer is the answer that reflects the truth while being sensitive not to turn off the interviewer. You should practice these answers in test interviews. Find someone you trust to ask you these questions and then reply with the answer that works for you. Do not respond with answers that sound too mechanical or as if you have memorized the response. You need to sound conversational and relaxed. You need to appear natural in your responses to questions.

Remember your brand positioning and the discussion I shared with you in Chapter One. What is it? How do you work it into the conversation to stay on message? It will be important to stay on message throughout the process so that you reinforce who you are at every opportunity. Now with the warning and reminder behind us, let's look at the key questions and some illustrative responses to them.

1. Where do you see yourself in five years?

This question is asked in most interviews. An inexperienced interviewer usually asks this question. Most young people do not know exactly where they will be in five years. In fact, most experienced people know that the world has changed and few senior people (and few interviewers) know where they will be in five years.

Of course, you have to answer this question even if it is not a great question. You might offer responses such as "Working in a company, like this one, that challenges me and fosters my professional growth" or "Continuing to build on my base of knowledge about this industry." Do not indicate that you expect to be still working at the company. It is not likely to be very believable since most entry-level people rarely stay at the same company for five years.

2. What are your strengths?
3. What is your greatest strength?
4. What are your weaknesses?
5. What is your greatest weakness?

Variations of these four questions are asked at almost every interview. It is almost as if all interviewers have gone to Interviewer Class 101 and were told to ask these questions.

You need to strike a reasonable and credible balance in your response. Most students have several strengths and at least a few weaknesses. You need to discuss the strengths that you understand are most relevant to the job based on your earlier research. Discuss the weaknesses that are *most irrelevant* to success on the job.

Most jobs require a broad array of skills. What did you learn in your research that is most important to the employer? If it is analytical skills, then discuss your analytical skills, your problem solving, and your use of software programs that are used in analysis. If it is creative skills, then focus on how innovative you are and how much you thrive in idea generation exercises.

Unacceptable responses concerning your strengths are answers such as "I have so many, I do not know where to begin", "Do you have an hour, because this will take a long time", or "I have too many strengths. In what area would you like me to focus?"

Some generic responses apply to most job situations for entry-level college graduates. Most employers want people who are attentive to detail, well organized, and work well with other people. If any of these traits apply to you then you should elaborate upon them.

Answering the question with regard to your weakness is always the tougher challenge. Never respond with "I have no weaknesses." Shape your response to what you believe is not required to do the job. As you discuss your weakness, do not spend too much time on the topic.

There are some safe responses to this question. Saying, "I probably set the bar too high at times, not everything needs to be perfect, but I would rather overachieve than miss an objective" will usually be accepted. "I sometimes try to do too much, but I am learning how to better gauge what needs to be done within a given time frame" is also a reasonable response.

Other responses that I have heard students use and which should be avoided include "I do not tolerate the mistakes of other people" and "I am a big thinker and not big on the details."

6. Can you please describe a situation in which you failed at something?

The employer wants to know how you handled failure. Pick something that taught you a lesson, but is not directly relevant to the job. Acceptable responses are "I did not make the soccer team. I still play soccer however, just not on the team." "I learned that we all cannot be great at everything."

Avoid noting that you failed a class such as English or Math unless it is a class that is totally irrelevant to the job requirements. Some students might say that they did not get along with a roommate. Avoid that response because it may raise a concern about your ability to work with others.

7. What do you do in your spare time?
8. What turns you on?
9. What turns you off?
10. How would your friends describe you?

These four questions assess what makes you tick and what gets you excited. An employer may be looking to see if you are a good match for the organizational culture. In addition, to borrow an expression, are you someone that the employer would want to "have a beer with" after work. Not literally of course, but employers will want to know if you will be a joy to have around the workplace. Advice concerning your response to these questions is that you want to get a sense if the corporate culture is a good fit for you. You should know if you want to have a beer (or if you do not drink, have a cup of coffee) with the people that work at the company.

Answers to these questions should express the real you so the likelihood of a match can be better assessed by both you and the employer. Still, use good common sense. Avoid responses that provide more information about you than is necessary. Safe yet good responses can relate to the favorite movies you like to see, the books you read, your favorite foods, or rooting for the popular home sports team (and never root against them as some people take their loyalty to the local team very seriously). Any activities related to gambling or dangerous adventures should not be discussed at this point. Friday night poker or bungee jumping might be fine with some people but it is best to avoid topics such as these until you have the job offer.

11. How do you respond to stress?

Very few employment situations come without moments of some kind of stress. It may not occur every day or every week, but stressful moments will happen. Employers do not always appreciate the amount of stress that a typical college student experiences. As a result, employers may be concerned about how you may respond to stress.

College students are under constant stress. Stress to fit in, get good grades, maintain a social life, part-time job, family issues, mounting debt and an assortment of a variety of other challenges are all part of a day in the life of many students. Without detailing all of the trials and tribulations that you experience, this is your invitation to let the employer know you can handle stress.

Do not be casual about it or boastful about it, but be sure to convey your ability to cope with it. Answers that are reasonable include "I have been working under quite a lot of stress all year and I have learned to not allow it to fog my thinking" or "I have a couple of very demanding professors who create stress and I have learned to take a deep breath and move forward." Avoid responses such as "It rolls down my back" or "I live for stress" because these are just not believable responses in most cases.

12. How do you respond to "unfair" criticism?

This question is used to determine whether you can handle feedback that you do not think is justified. It is a sign of maturity for someone to remain calm in the face of unjust feedback. Unfortunately, not all criticism in the workplace is justified and yet, everyone must press on and seek to get along.

Reasonable responses to this question include "I do not like it, but I have to consider it seriously. While it may not be justified in my opinion, it is still worth reflecting upon." Alternatively, "I do not expect to always be on the receiving end of fair and objective feedback and so, when I get criticism I do not agree with, I move on from there and do not let it upset me."

Inappropriate responses include such answers as "I ignore it" or "I just laugh it off in the person's face."

13. How have you handled a difficult professor?

14. How have you handled a difficult roommate?

These two questions are intended to assess how you interact with difficult people. Professors and roommates are among the most frequently encountered difficult people you will meet in a collegiate setting. Once employed in the workplace, you will periodically encounter difficult people there too. Your answers to these questions are important. It is best to communicate a level of tolerance toward difficult people without allowing them to obstruct progress.

A good answer is to say, "I know that the world is full of people who do not always wake up on the right side of the bed, but they may still have much to offer. When I was in college, I tried to see the best in people and not allow some of their less attractive moments to get in the way of what they have to offer." You can also add, "Almost everyone, if they work at it, can find something in common that they share with someone else even if that other person is a difficult person to work with. Something in common can be a basis for building a relationship."

15. What was your favorite course in college and what did you learn from it?

16. What was your least favorite course in college and what did you learn from it?

These questions are asked to determine what you learned and how relevant it is to the job. These questions are somewhat similar to the questions about your greatest strength and your greatest weakness. You need to match your answer to what you expect the employer is looking for in terms of skills on the job.

In terms of courses, you probably took more than 40 courses during your college career. Identify one or two courses that were your favorite. You can note that your series of courses in a particular field were all your favorite courses.

Relate the reason the course or courses were your favorite to what you are looking for in a job and what matches the job you are seeking. If you enjoy scientific exploration and the job you want is related to that area, then that is a perfect match. You can state, "I love to discover new things and that is why I loved those courses." If the job you are seeking requires working with a team, you can pick a course that entailed student collaboration in groups and note that as the reason for your love of the course.

Your least favorite course can be based on a professor who taught a class. It is quite common for students to have a least favorite professor. It is best to pick a course that is not relevant to the job you are seeking. For example, think of required freshman courses. Sometimes, these are very irrelevant to an applied area or profession and often a good response to the least favorite course question.

17. Did you like or dislike working in student groups in college?

Work in most companies requires that you often collaborate with other people in your department or in other departments. You need to embrace this form of activity and the employer needs to see that you do. A good response is "I love working with other people, and although I work well on my own, I enjoy the energy produced by the give and take in working with others."

18. What is your greatest accomplishment in college?

Employers want to determine what it is that you think is the greatest benefit to receiving a degree. There are varieties of acceptable responses to this question. For a job that may require you to multitask, it would be good to say "Getting good grades while meeting my many other obligations and working part-time at the same time. I had a heavy load throughout most of my college years." For a job that requires analytical thinking and problem solving, a good response is "Learning to consider all aspects to an issue and developing the skill to weigh the pros and the cons."

It is never a good idea to be glib or flip in your responses to any of the questions and this one in particular. Unacceptable responses include "Just getting out of there", "Surviving senior year", or "Passing algebra."

19. How has college changed you?

The question as to how college has changed you should be linked to what you consider to be one of your strengths. In particular, be sure that it is a strength that is relevant to the job requirements. Refer to the answers to the greatest strength questions at the beginning of this section.

20. Why do you want to work at our company?

This is a question designed primarily to see if your reason for working is based solely on the need to earn some money or if you have a professional reason to work at the company. Do you have a passion for the profession or industry in which the company operates? The employer wants to know the answer to this question and your response will reveal much about your motivations to work at the company.

Acceptable answers to this question include "The work you do builds on my education and skills", "People I respect speak very highly of the company and its management", or "I think the company has a bright future and I want to be a part of it." Answers which are not acceptable include "I need the money", "My boy friend has moved to the area and I want to be close to him", or "I am not sure if I have finalized an interest in working at your company and that is why I am here to find out more about you."

21. How much do you know about our company?
22. How much do you know about our industry?

These questions reflect the employer's interest in assessing if you have done your homework. The employer is interested in knowing if your decision to seek a job at the company is a well informed decision. If you have conducted the situation analysis described in Chapter Two, you will be ready to answer this question.

Good responses to these questions include "I have been reading about your company and discussing it with people who know something about it" or "I know about your stated goals and objectives and something about your competition, but I am sure that there is more to learn."

It is also acceptable to admit that you do not know everything about the company or its industry. You can say "I have discussed your company as a potential employer with friends and with my professor, but I would like to know more about it" or "I have been reading reports about the industry and competition and have a sense of some of its challenges, but I would like to learn more. I view it as an important industry."

Do not convey a sense that you know all there is to know or that you have not had time to study the company and its industry. Avoid responses such as "I know all I need to know at this time" or "I have not yet had the time to study your industry."

23. What do you think of our products?

24. What do you think of our advertising?

25. What do you think of our website?

26. What do you think of our stores?

27. What do you think of our press releases?

28. What do you think of the media coverage that we have been getting?

29. What do you think about the speech our President gave last week?

This is another set of questions employers use to determine if you did your research. The difference between these questions and some of the questions noted above relates to determining more than how much you know. It relates to assessing whether or not you have a point of view about some of these aspects of the company. The company knows that you are not an expert on any of the matters noted above, but the interviewer may use these questions to determine how strong your evaluative and analytical skills are through your response to these questions.

This is a very delicate set of questions and you need to give very careful thought to the answers. It may be that one of the people interviewing you had a major role in developing some part of these aspects of the company. The best preparation is to be sure that you have reviewed substantial information about the company that is publicly available. If you conducted the research about the company that was suggested in Chapter Two, you should be able to respond with relevant answers.

Reasonable answers could include responses such as "Yes, I have reviewed your website", "Yes, I visited some of your stores", or "Yes, I read the speech by the President of the company." Note some of the objective elements you observed in your preparation for the interview, such, as "I noticed that your website had a lengthy Privacy Policy listed on it", "I see you have three stores in our city", or "I see that the President made that speech before the Chamber of Commerce." Do not offer great praise or negative comments. If pressed, you can note that based on your review, it (the website/the stores/the speech) appeared professional. You can leave it at that.

There is one exception to this set of recommendations. The exception is that you should come to the interview with a point of view about the job function for which you are being interviewed. If the interview is for a position as a member of the President's speechwriting team, you need to come with a point of view about the speeches you have read. If you hope to be hired to work in a store, you need to have a point of view about the stores that you have visited. You should discuss very carefully, however, all other points of view about matters which you do not yet have the qualifications to assess.

30. Which competitor do you think we should be most worried about?

This is also a question to determine how much you know about the company and its industry. It is too early in the process to take a position that may not be accurate or well received. It is best to say, "I have learned that all competitors can be a challenge and should be monitored so that they do not become a problem, but I do not have access to enough information to single one out over the others." Another acceptable answer is to say, "Given how fast things can change in this world, no competitor can be ignored." Avoid responses such as "I do not think any of them are as good as you" or "With a company like your company, there is nothing to worry about."

31. What other jobs are you considering?

This represents part of the dance employers do with candidates. The employer is seeking to figure out who needs whom more. You can assume that the employer is interviewing other candidates and is looking to assess if you too are also looking at other opportunities. Try to appear that you need to be sought after and that you are not desperate. You also want to be sure to convey genuine interest in the job opportunity.

In effect, you need to strike a delicate balance between you are interested, but not desperate. A response such as "Of course I am looking at a number of options, but I am here because of a particular interest in this company" will usually satisfy this question. Do not tell them that you have no other options or that you are so determined to work for the employer that you have not looked at any other opportunities. Such statements will not get you any respect and may put you at a disadvantage in your negotiations with the company.

32. Why has it taken you so long to find a job?

If you have not landed a job within 3 or 4 months after graduation, some employers might wonder why you have not been successful in finding employment. They might ask this question to identify any problems with your candidacy that they have not yet identified. They may be concerned that you had already found a job, but that it did not work out and now they want to know why it did not work out. They may have reservations that you could be less than interested in working in a full time capacity and are not serious about looking for a job.

There are many legitimate reasons why a graduate may not have found employment. Family obligations, travel through Europe, volunteer work are just a few of the possible reasons you may not have found something. What you can say in response to this question is "I have been selective about the job opportunities I have examined and I am pleased to have only recently learned about this one."

33. If we hire you, how will we be better off?

This question has a number of objectives for the employer. First, the employer wants to be certain he has not overlooked some important aspect of what you have to offer. The employer also wants to observe how you see yourself contributing. It is best to be somewhat humble. Remember that you are not being hired to become the president of the company, but simply a new and likely entry-level employee.

A suitable response is to say, "Well, I am sure that the company has many people who are contributing and I would be one of many, but you will be better off because I expect to do everything I can to make a difference to our work together." What you do not say is "I will earn my salary back and then some" or "I guarantee a strong return on your investment in me." Do not over promise and appear arrogant.

34. Now that I have described it to you, why do you want this particular job?

Your response to this question will be shaped by what you have heard in the interview up to this point in time. You will need to have digested enough information so you can provide a fair and accurate response. If you are sure that the employer is looking for a particular attribute in a job candidate and if it accurately reflects who you are, this becomes a good opportunity to play back the attribute. For example, if you have heard in the interview the company is seeking a person who is a self-starter and if that is who you are, you can say "I like the idea of being able to start my own initiatives and not wait to be told what to do all the time."

On the other hand, if you are not sure what you think at this point and you wish to reflect on the entire conversation, it is acceptable to say "I think it fits well with my interests and skills" or "I like the way you have described my expected responsibilities, this is what I have been looking to do." Avoid making it appear that the interviewer has not done a good job. You can also say, "I am very interested, but I have a few more questions."

35. Based on our description of the job, what do you think about it?

The first thing to know about an answer to this question is that unless the job appears like the last job on the planet you would ever consider, do not close the door to this opportunity. You may find that after learning more about it, even if you do not initially find it something you want, you could change your mind.

Remember that one of the most important attributes you can convey in an interview is enthusiasm. This question provides you with an opportunity to share your enthusiasm for the company and possibly for the position. Of course, if you are not interested in the position at this point, you can simply be polite and indicate that the position sounds interesting without saying you do not want the job. If you do want the job, you need to convey positive feelings and appear very interested in it. Employers know that they can train people to do most jobs, but they also know they cannot easily invest passion in someone who does not have it. Employers are looking for some passion in job candidates.

This question also opens the door for you to ask a question. You can say, "I am very interested, but I have a few questions."

The employer will understand and will likely appreciate it that you care enough to ask an intelligent question.

36. If we offered you a different job, would you take it?

Employers ask this question for a number of reasons. You may have impressed them, but you may not be the lead candidate. They may have another position for you in the organization. It may also be a way for them to determine how much you care about the specific position as opposed to the company itself.

During the interview, you want to appear as caring about the position. You do not want to be perceived as willing to take any job. You also want to appear flexible or caring enough about the organization. A good response can be "It would depend on the nature of the different job and how close it matches my skills and interests." Another response might be to say, "I would need to know more about the other job before being able to make a decision, but I am very interested in this organization."

An unacceptable response is "I really want the job I came here to discuss with you and would rather not discuss anything else at this time." Importantly, short answers such as "Yes" or "No" will not work in response to this question. You need to convey a more middle of the road and flexible position while still indicating you very much prefer the job you came to discuss.

37. If we offer you this job, how long do you intend to stay?

This may appear to be a ridiculous question. Who would say forever? Who would say a year? There is a reason to ask it that serves the interests of the employer. Your answer to this question provides the employer with a sense of your long term plans. In fact, it provides a good sense if you have any plan at all. They also want to know you are not likely to be a job hopper going from job to job. They would like to see a return on their investment in employees they hire and train.

Clearly, you will not know how long you will stay since you have not yet started the job and experienced what it is like to work at the company. A reasonable answer is to say, "I want to learn as much as possible and as long as I feel I am learning and growing, then I intend to stay." Another possible response is to say, "I want to develop relationships and I know to do so takes a number of years and that is my current sense of how long I will stay." This provides the employer with an impression you are a serious person with a plan and that is an attractive attribute to convey.

38. Do you have any questions for us?

This question is usually asked toward the end of an interview. It is always a good sign if they ask you this question because it is not often asked of a candidate who is not considered a strong candidate. If they are asking you this question toward the end of the interview, that is encouraging. You still may not receive a job offer because the person asking the question may not yet have received feedback from other colleagues who interviewed you. Still, it is a good sign.

There are questions you should be prepared to ask. First, you should come prepared with a handful of questions in anticipation you might be asked this question. Questions worth asking are questions related to the general nature of the company's business, such as "Where do you see growth opportunities in the future" or "How do you see your division's objectives changing in the future."

Obviously, if during the course of your interview these topics were covered, you do not need to ask these questions. You can ask the interviewers to elaborate on their previous answers, such as "You said earlier that you do not see as much growth in certain areas of the country or certain departments, could you please tell me more about that?" If someone said something and at the time, you did not want to interrupt with a question, then this is the time to ask your question. As an example, you can ask, "Earlier you indicated that the job is likely to take on additional responsibilities in the future, could you tell me more about that?"

If you think that you have created rapport with the person who is interviewing you, there is yet another set of questions to ask. You can ask, "What has been your secret to success in the company (or profession)" or "What do you think is the single most important factor to succeed in your company given your success?" The key to effectively asking these questions is to be sure you do not appear patronizing and so, be sure you have created enough rapport in the interview before asking these questions.

There are also questions that address the next steps in the selection process. Even if they do not ask you if you have any questions, it is important that you ask these questions. They include such questions as "What do you see the next step in the process of your hiring decision", "When can I next expect to hear from you", or "When do you expect to make a hiring decision?" Some people may think that these questions are overly aggressive. Far from being pushy, these questions reflect your interest in the job. In addition, you have now invested your time and have a right to know how the process will unfold.

Consider one final note about these questions. Never ask "When can I start" or "How did I do?" While on the one hand, asking these kinds of questions indicates an appealing level of self-confidence, they also potentially convey a level of arrogance that should be avoided.

39. How much money are you expecting to earn/what kind of starting salary are you looking for?

This question may emerge during an initial telephone interview. In the next chapter, I will share some tips with you about how to negotiate for a salary and other compensation. If you are asked this question toward the end of the face-to-face interview, it is usually a good sign. It means that you are worth the time to start that discussion.

Some students are so desperate for a job that they may respond with the answer "I will take anything" or "Whatever the job pays." Avoid those responses. Remember that most employers are not excited about hiring desperate people. Their thinking is that if you are desperate and other employers have not shown an interest in you then they may be making a mistake offering you a position.

It is best to keep it slightly vague at this point. Be sure that they want you before starting your salary negotiations and you will not likely be at that point yet. You can respond by saying, "I am flexible and would expect the going market rate for this position." You can also note, "I would need to know more about the entire benefit package and your system for promotions and raises before sharing a hard number with you." In either case, you can include a comment that while salary is important to you, you are most interested in the total package and the room to grow with the company.

40. When can you start?

Be realistic in your response to this question. Many students are eager to get on with their lives and earn money immediately. There is a natural tendency to say you can start tomorrow. If you can start immediately, you should expect to be taken up on your offer. Never tell the employer that you can start today or tomorrow if you cannot do it. It may cost you the job.

Even if you can start the next day after an offer is made, it is usually good to get all of your loose ends in order before you start the job. Most employers understand that you will have other obligations to address before you start your job. Few will expect you to start within 24 hours. If an employer demands that you start right away, you should be somewhat concerned how well the employer is managing its business. The best way to answer this question is to ask the question "How soon do you need me" and do so by telling the employer you would like to clear your schedule so that you can start the job in two weeks or so.

In answering this question understanding that you have other obligations that may not be able to be resolved in a day or two., be sure to provide current employers, even part-time employers, with the customary two weeks notice expected by most employers. If your new employer does not want to wait for you to provide adequate notice, you should be somewhat concerned about the new employer's values. The new employer should know better and should be

USING THESE QUESTIONS AND ANSWERS

These questions and the suggested answers to them are just a start in helping you make a sale. Your research about the companies you want to work at will likely lead you to your own custom list of questions that are relevant to the interview situation. The longer your list of potential questions and answers, the better prepared you will be. Importantly, the better prepared you are the more confident you will be. Your confidence is likely to be noticed by the employer, increasing your chances you will receive a job offer.

The importance of selling yourself cannot be overstated. In a recent story reported in the New York Times, a young man reported being turned down by many employers until he began selling himself. His observations were full of insight. He noted "Looking back, I see what I did wrong. I had an outdated way of thinking about the interview process. I didn't provide any detail, I didn't talk about how I saw the industry, and I didn't offer any tips on how they could improve their online presence. I was doing the bare minimum instead of trying to sell myself." Unlike that young man, you now have an appreciation and knowledge about the need to sell yourself. You know you need to go beyond the "bare minimum" in your preparation.

Now, let's turn our attention to getting the job offer and closing the sale.

CHAPTER FOUR

Getting the Offer:
Closing the Sale

"You can get everything in life you want
if you will just help enough other people get what they want"
Zig Ziglar

Marketing professionals invest significant resources in building relationships with customers. They understand their best future customer may be someone who has been a customer in the past. Career building is also a relationship building process. After you have completed the interviews, there is still much work to be done. You need to identify opportunities to build relationships with the people you meet during your interviews.

NEXT STEP AFTER AN INTERVIEW

After leaving an interview, you should do two things immediately. First, within a few minutes following the interview, you should sit down and take notes. Record any interesting comments made by the people you met with during the course of the interview. Also, record your responses to questions you answered during the interview. Note taking will help you remember how you answered some of the questions posed to you. It will provide you with an opportunity to reflect on your responses and decide how you might modify your answers in the future in response to similar questions. You might want to review your answers with someone you trust to determine if your answers were effective.

You may have an opportunity on another occasion to speak with some of the people you meet during the interview. A good set of notes will allow you to contribute more to the next conversation. In addition, people will be impressed that you remembered things they mentioned during the first meeting

The second and most important task to accomplish after completing a set of interviews is to send a thank you note to the people you met during the interviews. They gave up a part of their day to spend time with you. In some cases, they may have been doing a favor for a colleague in scheduling time to see you. In all cases, you need to send each person a note of appreciation for meeting with you.

In Chapter Three, I recommended that you collect a business card from each person you meet during interviews. If someone doesn't have a business card, I suggested that you write down the person's contact information. You will use this information to send your thank you notes.

Notice that I did not recommend sending an email to any of the people you meet. While sending an email to thank someone is acceptable, it doesn't set you apart from everyone else. Sending a thank you in the form of a note does separate you from the crowd. I recommend you arrive at the interview with a set of thank you cards that already have your return address and a stamp on them. Some students use note cards that have their name printed on the outside of the card. These make a professional image and you should consider doing it too. Remember to keep the graphic style on the printed note cards or thank you cards consistent with your business card, cover letter, and resume.

The note should be hand written and brief. It's best to keep it three to five sentences long. Ideally, the note will refer to something that was said during the interview. It could include something you found to be insightful or informative. You could also reference an observation you made to the person during your interview. Perhaps you discovered that you share a common interest or acquaintance. Give this note much thought.

Bring a blank piece of paper with you. Take a minute to practice writing the note in draft form before actually writing the note card you will be sending. Do all you can to avoid sloppy handwriting and bring a pocket dictionary with you if spelling is occasionally a challenge.

The notes you send should not be copies of each other. People at the company will sometimes compare notes received from job candidates and you want them to know you took the time to send them a personalized note. Once you write these notes, find a mailbox within a block or two of the employer's location and mail them. Your thank you notes will likely arrive within one to two days, keeping you and your job interest fresh in the minds of the people who interviewed you.

As you construct your notes, decide if you will use the first name or last name of the individual. Use the person's first name if you were told during the interview to use a first name or if you developed enough rapport during the interview to do so. Here are some examples of acceptable notes students have sent to people they met during an interview:

Dear Mary,

Thank you so much for taking time to talk to me yesterday. While I was very excited about your industry before we met, your vision of the business makes me even more encouraged about the future. Please feel free to contact me with any questions you may have. I look forward to our next conversation.

Dear Mr. Johnson,

Thank you for your time yesterday. It sure is a small world. We both know Tom Smith at the driving range. I hope his instruction to you has been as good as what he has shared with me. He is a great golf instructor. In terms of your company, I remain eager to move to the next step in our discussions. I will keep my schedule open to talk further with you when you are ready.

Dear Peter,

Thank you for spending time with me yesterday. I enjoyed meeting you and everyone at your company. It is clear that you all like your work. On a personal note, you and I may be the only Dolphins fans in New England. We will have to stay in touch about where to find the best place to cheer for the 'Fins on Sundays. Regardless of how things turn out, please stay in touch.

Dear Ms. Jones,

Thanks for your time yesterday. I followed up on your suggestion to review the recent edition of the paper that analyzes the future of the industry. I agree the future appears challenging, but your firm looks like it will be one of the few to survive. On a personal note, I picked up the book you suggested to help me with my travel plans to Africa. I hope to speak to you soon!

These notes blend your continued interest in the company with something personal that may have emerged during the discussions. It's important to end the notes with a reference to your continued interest in the position.

MAINTAINING CONTACT AFTER THE INTERVIEW

Students frequently ask how soon they should follow up with a prospective employer after they have completed an interview. That's a good question. The answer will depend on what the interviewer(s) told you. At the conclusion of an interview, you should always ask the employer when you should expect to hear back about the company's hiring decision. You should ask about the next steps in the process.

Schedule your follow up according to what the employer tells you about the interview process. If the potential employer provides you with a specific date, it's usually best not to inquire on that day or the day after that date if you haven't yet been contacted. Don't seem too eager or desperate for a response. You also don't want to convey the sense that you're "high maintenance," requiring substantial feedback. At the same time, you shouldn't let too much time elapse beyond the date you were provided.

It's usually a good practice to allow a few days beyond the date given before following up with the employer. I always suggest calling rather than sending an email. Emails sometimes are deleted accidently or end up in a spam folder. You want to find an opportunity to interact with the employer, and the telephone is the best way to do this.

Don't leave a message if the person doesn't answer the phone. Leaving a message removes the opportunity to interact. You want to maximize the chances of communicating. Interaction can fast forward relationship building and you might get a better sense of how things are or are not moving forward.

Successful salespeople know that the best time to call is either first thing in the morning, before the official start of business, or just after the official business hours are over. Those times are usually the best to reach your contacts on the telephone. However, if you've called on several occasions and have not been able to reach the person on the telephone, you may have to leave a message to keep your candidacy fresh in the mind of your contact at the potential employer's business.

Your participation in the interview process is a first major step in building a relationship with the people you meet during the interview. There are a few more things you can do to build relationships. For example, if you know there is an industry-related function in your area that will likely be attended by some of the people you met, you might want to attend. They will appreciate that you are a professional who invests time in keeping up with developments in your field.

If there is a conference or a lecture at your college that might be of interest, you should consider extending an invitation to people you want to get to know better. The topic doesn't have to be 100 percent relevant to your area of interest. It can be a cultural event the person might find of interest. Even if your invitation is not accepted, it will be appreciated.

You can also monitor news stories related to your industry or profession of interest. You should be doing this anyway in order to keep up on current events. When you find an item in the news you think will be of interest to people you met during the interview, send an email to them with a link to the story. Consider offering a brief point of view about the story to demonstrate how immersed you are in the subject area.

There are a few things you should not do. While an occasional email or invitation is acceptable in order to stay on people's radar, it's important to be professional and appropriate. Don't under any circumstances send a joke via email or something you think the recipient will find humorous. Humor can backfire, and you probably don't know the people well enough to share humorous items. It also undercuts your position as a candidate who is serious about wanting to work at this particular company.

Don't immediately attempt to "friend" them on a social networking website. They may someday become "friends," but don't rush the process. Moreover, under no circumstances should you drop by for an unannounced visit at the company. Your unannounced arrival, no matter how much rapport you developed during the interview, is unlikely to be viewed favorably.

HOW TO RESPOND TO REJECTION

I have a prediction. It's based on many years of observing the outcome of the job search process. Most people don't receive a job offer from prospective employers they have contacted for a job. It is likely that some prospective employers will reject you. You may receive several rejections before you receive a job offer that meets your needs. There is a good reason for my prediction. Even in a good economy, each open job usually has many people applying for it. If 20 people apply for a job, 19 people will be rejected.

Jobs that are highly coveted can have hundreds or even thousands of applicants. In these cases, of course, the number of rejections extends into the range of hundreds or thousands. If you apply the marketing tactics that I have shared with you in Chapters One and Two, you will likely apply to many jobs. Therefore, you are likely to receive a number of rejection letters or in some cases, no letter at all.

Since rejections are likely to occur, how do you respond to them? How you respond will depend how far you progressed in the screening process. If you had some contact with a company representative either by telephone or in person, even rejection is a relationship building opportunity. At the beginning of this chapter, I noted that marketing professionals emphasize relationship building in all they do. You can even build a relationship out of a rejection!

If you are rejected for a job, send the person a brief note. Tell him or her you appreciate the time devoted to your application. Include a statement you wish the interviewer well and you hope he or she stays in touch with you.

If your contact with the company extended beyond a telephone call and progressed to a face-to-face interview, you can also take this opportunity to contact the people you met during the interview. Consider sending each person a note expressing your appreciation for the time spent considering your candidacy. Connect with the people you met by contacting them on LinkedIn or some other social networking site. You have nothing to lose in doing so other than a few minutes of your time.

The people who receive your notes and contacts will not be upset with you. Far from it, they will be impressed you cared enough to maintain contact and there are no hard feelings. Some of the people who were part of the candidate selection process may have liked you better than the candidate chosen for the job. It's possible that a few months later, the person who took the job may leave or may be asked to leave. If you use your rejection to build on your relationships, you may be the candidate that the company approaches the next time a job becomes available.

REFERENCE CHECKING

An important aspect of any marketing program is to have a credible set of endorsements. In the case of marketing your candidacy for a job, that translates into a credible set of references. In thinking about whom you will ask to be a reference, you will need to address a number of criteria. The people you approach should meet as many of the following criteria as possible:

- They are familiar with your strengths and weaknesses.
- They have known you a long time and at least for more than a year.
- They are supporters of your candidacy for a particular job.
- They can be counted on to return a phone call by the prospective employer within 24 hours.

Before briefly looking at each of these criteria, you may notice there is something missing from this set of criteria. Some students feel that it's important that their references are people who are famous or who occupy important positions. If the person you include is famous or important, that's great. Except in the case of a few positions, however, it's best not to include someone as a reference unless that person substantially meets the criteria set forth above. What good is it to have a famous person on your reference list if Mr. or Ms. Fame doesn't return a telephone call from a reference checker or if the person says he or she hardly knows you?

Let's examine the criteria one at a time. The reference checker is almost always going to ask your reference about your greatest strength and greatest weakness. What have you been telling prospective employers when they ask you about your strengths and weaknesses? You need to get your reference on the same page with you in terms of how they might respond.

Preparing your reference for a reference check is important. In some cases, the reference may be a professor whose class you took in junior year. The person may know you, but not as well as he or she needs to know you. The reference may also be someone who's not in your field of interest. Share as much as possible with your reference to assure there is consistency in the communications about you.

The person whom you select may be someone who is asked to serve as a reference for many other students. Refresh the person's memory of what you are capable of doing and your experience. Begin by sharing your resume with your prospective references. They will learn things about you in reviewing your resume they didn't know. Provide a description of the type of jobs you are seeking and the companies you are approaching for employment. Take the key questions from Chapter Three and provide your reference with the answers you have given or expect to give in interviews. Your references may not review all of the materials you provide in detail, but whatever they review will result in a better reference from them.

There are common questions your references will likely be asked. Potential employers may ask about your attendance and punctuality, your work ethic, how well you work with others, how attentive to detail you are, and how well you work under pressure. Discuss each of these areas with your references so that the answers they provide are reasonably consistent with the answers you might also provide in an interview.

In terms of how long someone knows you, again, it is best you know each other for at least a year. Asking a professor who had you in only one class during the most recent and perhaps, your last semester at college is not the best idea. If it's all you have to work with, it will have to do. However, you're always better off picking a reference who has known you for a long time.

In discussing your candidacy with your references, don't be subtle. Be direct and ask them if they think you would be a good candidate for the jobs you are seeking. Ask them if they can respond to a reference request within 24 hours. Their willingness to allow you to provide their cell phone number is a way to assess how quickly they will respond.

Always have more references ready to assist you than you may think you need. Some references may be a better fit for certain opportunities. In addition, you should not overwork any one single reference. The person may lose some enthusiasm if called upon too often on your behalf. Finally, remember that references are not always equally available. The busy season for one reference may be a slow season for another. Arrange it so that your prospective employer can reach at least two of your references quickly. The reference checking should not drag on too long. It could cost you the job.

SALARY NEGOTIATION

One of the most delicate aspects of your job search emerges after all reference checking is completed. Sometimes it even occurs before reference checking begins. It's the salary negotiation. The company wants to hire you or it wouldn't start a salary discussion. You want to work at the company or you wouldn't have taken the interview process this far. What makes the salary negotiation so delicate is that it's an area in which your goal and the company's goal diverge. You probably want as much money as possible. Generally, the company wants to pay you as little as possible. Many students begin their salary research by referring to national benchmarks that list salaries for different majors or different types of jobs. These can be helpful sources of information about how much you can expect to earn starting out. A very good source of such information can be found on government websites. In particular, review material available at the Bureau of Labor statistics (http://www.bls.gov). You can also check with your college career counselors who often have relevant starting salary information. I discussed NACE in Chapter One. It also provides some salary information your career counselor may be able to access on your behalf.

You must use this off-the-shelf salary information carefully. The information is usually not granular enough. It reflects national averages or at best, averages in your region. It usually doesn't reflect your community. The salary range can be quite broad and not a good basis for indicating the salary you should expect for a position with a specific employer. In addition, quoting a salary survey to a prospective employer demanding that the employer meet the average salary is not going to work for you. Don't pressure prospective employers by waving a salary survey in your hand. If you do, you will likely leave empty handed—except for your salary survey.

Regardless of what the averages may be for salaries in your discipline and geographic area, most companies have set salary limits or ranges that aren't easily changed. The larger the company, the more likely it has set salary ranges that your potential new boss cannot change. When a company offers you a starting salary, the amount has likely been approved by the hiring manager, that person's supervisor, and the human resources department. Getting that amount increased is a very difficult task. While it's possible, don't assume the amount can or will be changed no matter how good of a candidate you are.

You'll receive all kinds of advice from many sources about how to structure what may be your first real salary negotiation. I'll offer my own advice and a rationale for it. Keep in mind throughout the negotiating process, you have two objectives that may come into conflict.

Your first objective is to earn enough money to meet your financial obligations. Accepting a salary that is less than what it takes to meet your obligations will only add stress to your life. It also can impact your job performance because if you are not able to afford your living arrangements, you will not be very happy with your job. However, asking for too high a salary may remove you from consideration for the job. Employers may conclude you're too expensive. Even if they are willing to compromise and raise their offer, they may be concerned you'll leave the company when something better comes along.

Your second objective is to get the job. You are interested in getting started on your career. The longer you hold out for a job that pays you what you want, the longer the time you aren't building your career. You are the only person who can appreciate your circumstances completely. Only you know fully your financial situation. Only you know how much you want the job that's being offered to you. As you receive advice on what salary to seek, steer your own ship concerning these matters and weigh the tradeoff between your financial needs and getting your career started.

To assist you in assessing this tradeoff or conflict, I want to share my own point of view with you. My bias is to sacrifice some short-term financial gain in order to get your career started. Assuming a position is offered to you that you want, but at a salary less than you are seeking, you need to assess how likely it is that a similar position will be offered to you in the near future at a higher salary level. If a position similar to the one offered to you is not likely to be available in the next few months, consider lowering your financial objectives to get your career moving and obtain some valuable professional experience.

There are things you can do to make the financial sacrifice tolerable. Many students continue to work evenings and weekends as waiters, servers, bartenders, or babysitters to supplement income during the first few years of professional life. Rather than turn down a job that may be a few thousand dollars less than you may need, you can consider supplementing your income with a part-time job so you don't have to turn down a professional job opportunity that in every other respect is the job you want.

If you perform well on the job, even in a poor economy, there may be opportunities to receive raises or promotions at your new employer. In addition, people no longer stay at their first job for as long as they may have twenty years ago. It's not uncommon for someone to have four or more jobs within the first six to seven years of working. A few of these job changes can mean a 10 to 20 percent increase in compensation. As a result, accepting a lower than desired starting salary is not a life sentence of poverty. It's just a short-term situation that will likely change in the first or second year of working.

Here is what you can expect in terms of the salary negotiations process. You'll be asked if you're still interested in the position and when you can start working. Remember to avoid agreeing to a start date that is too soon. The employer may revisit the question of your salary requirements. Unless something has radically changed in your life, you should be consistent in your answer. What you indicated in earlier conversations should be reflected in your response now.

If you're offered a salary below what you can accept, you should feel free to turn it down. Don't accept a salary with the idea that, if a better offer comes along in a few weeks of starting, you can leave and take that other, higher paying job. Your reputation is one of your greatest assets, and you don't want to jeopardize how people perceive you. If you start with an employer only to leave within a few weeks, your reputation will be damaged. The world is becoming a smaller place all the time through the use of various forms of communications channels. There is a good chance other employers may find out what you did, and you could find it more difficult to get a job somewhere else.

If you're offered a job, but the salary is too low, politely inform the employer it doesn't meet your needs. You can say, "I was hoping for more compensation than that, but I very much want to work with you. Is there any way you can increase your offer?" This way, you state you want to work for the company, and you want a salary level that works for both you and the employer. You can ask the employer how the two of you can work together to identify a salary level that both of you can accept.

Asking if there is room to improve upon the initial offer will help you test the upper limit of the offer. An employer's representative might be empowered by the organization to go slightly higher in terms of the salary offer. The person offering you the job might indicate the company can increase the offer.

Organizations vary in terms of when they will reevaluate the salary of a new employee. Some have schedules that are always adhered to and some are flexible. As a part of the negotiation, you can ask if your salary can be reviewed sooner than in accordance with the normal salary review process. A smaller organization is generally more flexible with regard to when it will review your work and consider a salary increase.

During the job offer conversation, you may be tempted to accept the job immediately. Don't give into temptation. Ask the employer if you can review the offer and provide your answer in a day or two. Most employers will understand you prefer to think about it and consider your reflection an effective deliberating decision-making style. Taking time to think over the offer conveys an impression you are not desperate. It also provides you with time to reflect upon the offer and arrive at the best decision in accepting or rejecting it.

You should provide your decision to the employer within the agreed upon time. Ask for a letter from the employer that documents the important elements of the job offer if you accept the job. These elements usually consist of salary, title, work responsibilities, work location, person who will be your supervisor, start date, and any other financial-related considerations agreed upon during the negotiations.

You should send a letter to the company representative confirming your receipt of its offer. Your acceptance letter usually can be sent in the form of an email unless you are requested by the employer to send it another way. Some employers may ask you to mail it back to them with your signature on the letter used to offer the job to you. The communication assures the legal aspects of an offer and an acceptance have occurred. This provides you with some security against the company rescinding the offer before you start the job.

INFORMING EVERYONE THAT YOU HAVE A JOB

An important consideration is what to do about other companies you have been in contact with concerning potential employment once you've accepted a position. At the beginning of this chapter, I emphasized how important it is to build relationships. Healthy business relationships are the foundation of effective marketing practice. It's so valuable that several thousand articles and books have been written addressing the techniques needed to build and maintain relationships.

You too are building relationships. The more successful you are at it, the more likely you will be able to leverage your relationship building into your next career move. Upon accepting a job, most students forget about the companies they have had interviews with or that have expressed an interest in them. You need to avoid being viewed like most college students.

Don't announce to anyone you have a job until you're actually on the job. People new to the workplace find it amazing a job offered to them can disappear before they start work. They are shocked when a company rescinds its offer of employment. These kind of unpleasant things do happen. My advice is to wait until you start your new job and have been working for a few weeks before announcing you have found a job.

Determine whether the job described to you during your initial interviews is turning out to be the job you are now doing. Once you have been on the job for a few weeks and you like it, you can tweet and update your status on your social networking sites to indicate you have a job. You should send notes (written notes using those same note cards mentioned earlier) to prospective employers you met with during your search to inform them you have accepted a position with another company.

In your notes to other employers, state your title, the division or business unit that you are working in, and a modest description of what you are doing. You can then take a step further in relationship building with these potential employers and seek connections with them on professional social networking sites such as LinkedIn. Some employers who have not yet offered you a job will immediately find you more interesting than before. Don't be surprised if they remain in contact with you and offer you a job after you have gathered more experience.

Don't forget to send thank you notes to the people who have helped you in your job search. Sending flowers, candy, or even a favorite bottle of wine to anyone who provided you with extra help will be appreciated. Thank each person who serves as a reference for you each time they do so. Once you actually start your job, consider providing a small gift to them. It is the right thing to do.

Prepare to change from a person who is a job candidate to a person who is a source of job referrals. You will likely continue to receive contacts from people with a job opening who do not know that you have accepted a job. Use these opportunities to refer other worthy candidates to employers contacting you. Everyone will appreciate your efforts.

FINAL WORDS ABOUT WAITING FOR A JOB OFFER

To the job candidate, every day that goes by without a job can feel like a week. Every week that goes by can feel like a month. This waiting may be difficult for you. Keeping in touch with job candidates is not usually the highest priority to the companies you have contacted.

While waiting for the job offer, students will often ask what's taking so long. Filling a job is important to a company or it wouldn't put the effort and expense into advertising job openings and meeting with people in order to decide whom to hire. However, company employees usually have many other responsibilities so that hiring you may not be at the top of their list of things to do.

While the time it takes to find a job will vary, you can control such things as starting salary requirements, willingness to relocate to another area, start date, and selectivity about the type of position and company you find acceptable. The more flexible you are on these matters, the sooner you will start working.

However, there are many things not in your control. The other issues that the companies you've contacted are addressing will often take priority over hiring you or any other candidates. In particular, your desired position is not the only position that companies are seeking to fill. As a result, you may have to wait longer than you would like to wait. You will need to be patient.

Some students just hang out at home, waiting for the telephone to ring. They may engage in heavy sunbathing at the local pool or beach. They may join their friends in starting their day at 10:00 p.m. and ending it at 4:00 a.m. after a night out at their favorite places where other people like them come together to swap stories about not having a job. My advice is to avoid these routines. Socializing with pals is great, but stay focused on your job search.

There are actions you can take while waiting to make you more valuable to prospective employers now and in the future. Working on polishing skills relevant to your potential job is a great way to spend your time before an offer arrives. For example, if computers are important in your area of interest and your skills are below average, attend a workshop that can help you improve your use of computers. Many other skills such as writing, fluency in a foreign language, or data analysis can be refined so that on future interviews, you can feel more confident about these skills when asked about them.

Although you may have graduated, learning should never stop. Consider taking an evening class at a local college that will add to your portfolio of skills. Increasingly, graduates return to school the summer after they graduate and attend a concentrated program of study in an area relevant to a job search. I have observed liberal arts majors who learn enough about information systems, business, or health care during a summer study program immediately after graduation to become reasonable candidates for entry-level jobs in those fields.

As noted earlier, you should also consider volunteering your time for a worthwhile cause or two during the time you are waiting. You will feel good about doing it. You may even make some friends or good professional contacts during the course of your volunteer work. And you will be gaining new work skills.

Doing an internship immediately after graduation can be a great way to increase your number of contacts and add to your skills. It is becoming increasingly common to find internships available to people who have already graduated. By working at an internship, when an employer asks you what you've been doing since graduation, you can reply you're doing more than working on a tan or meeting your friends for coffee at the local diner at 4:00 a.m.

There is one important thing to keep in mind during this time. Keep a positive attitude. I understand it can become harder to do as the calendar unfolds and you still don't have a job. However, people who meet you on job interviews will know if you have a positive outlook on life or not. The people you meet during your day-to-day activities will know it too. Nobody is excited about recommending someone with a negative attitude. Everyone wants to be with people who can smile, laugh, and approach life with a sunny disposition.

When you pause to think about all of this advice, I'm sure you'll find much to laugh about. Your job search is a process that can teach you many things about yourself and about life. Remember that eventually everyone gets a job. Everyone gets a chance—usually many chances—to define his or her place in the world through meaningful work. Your chance will come. When it does, be sure it finds you with a smile on your face.

Before we part company, I want to share an excerpt from a commencement address that captures the spirit of how I think you should go forward in your journey. Steve Jobs, the CEO of Apple, delivered wonderful parting words at the 2005 Stanford University Graduation ceremonies. His words provide a perspective on the way you should consider planning your future. No futures are certain. Your best guide about the future should be shaped by what *you* think. Here is a wonderful piece of wisdom from Mr. Jobs:

"Your time is limited, so don't waste it living someone else's life. Don't be trapped by dogma—which is living with the results of other people's thinking. Don't let the noise of others' opinions drown out your own inner voice. And most important, have the courage to follow your heart and intuition. They somehow already know what you truly want to become. Everything else is secondary."

Enjoy the experience!

APPENDIX

- How to Research a Business or Industry Sector

- Power Verbs

- Bibliography

HOW TO RESEARCH A BUSINESS OR INDUSTRY SECTOR

1. Determine the key word or words you will use to find the information. This is sometimes referred to as a search string. Your search string is the word or the set of words you put into Google, Yahoo!, or Bing when searching for information. To be thorough, you should use all three of these popular search engines. There are also search engines that specialize in specific disciplines or professions and you should seek to use them too. To be sure you have exhausted all possibilities, never use just one word or one set of words. Instead, try several potentially relevant words. For example, if your subject is Army advertising, then you should search using the words "army advertising", military recruiting", "army marketing, "army promotions", and so on. Notice that these words were placed within quotation marks. This is how most search engines accept a phrase to be searched (although some do not allow quotation marks. Try doing it both ways and see what you get back in terms of search results). Another technique is to try to add some additional words that are outside the quotation marks. Examples might be to add these types of words: data, trends, results, reports, statistics, information, awards, and performance. There are many possibilities and the more important the opportunity is to you, the more possibilities you should explore. The 4 two-word combinations above could each be coupled with any one of the eight words in the previous sentence. That would result in 32 different searches. It is very important to not just search for the company you are interested in, but also the competition. If you are interested in a subject rather than a company be sure to search on related subjects. For example, if Crime is your interest, try variations: white collar, white collar crime, violent crime, and so on.

2. Use the same search terms or strings developed in step one. You may use one of the search engines that combine

all other search engines. Sites such as dogpile.com, mamma.com, or vivisimo.com are great additional search engines to use. Using search engines is a good first step because it may reveal documents you can then find on the library database. Remember to click on the word "cached" when you arrive at a site that is no longer active. By clicking on cached, you can at least see what the page looked like before it went inactive. You can also visit Alexa.com and do the same thing (it archives old web pages).

3. Access the databases available to you. Your school library or the local public libraries are likely to have a wide variety of databases that can be accessed in the library and sometimes, from remote locations. The best databases for most employers and industries are described below. There are also specialized databases that focus on specific industry sectors and you should ask the librarian about the availability of these at your library. Use the search terms developed in step one. At the library, do not overlook any hard copy of relevant reference documents.

4. Identify relevant government bureaus, departments, and agencies that cover the subject you are interested in. Start with the websites of these government organizations so you will be better equipped to ask for specific information, most of which is usually free or very low cost. Contact them by phone (most have free 800 telephone numbers you can find on their websites.

5. Identify relevant government organizations, industry associations, foundations and institutes that cover the subject you are interested in. Start with the websites of these organizations so you will be better equipped to ask for specific information when you contact them by phone. Most of these organizations have free 800 telephone numbers you can find on their websites. The information is usually free or very low cost.

6. Identify the daily, weekly, and monthly publications that cover the subject you are interested in. Contact them by phone and check their websites for information.

7. Finally, if you are interested in a company, examine its website for information. Then contact the company's public relations or investor relations departments, which usually can provide certain information to you.

DATABASES TO CONSULT IN YOUR SEARCH FOR INFORMATION ARE THE FOLLOWING:

ABI/INFORM Global™ is one of the most comprehensive business databases on the market. It includes in-depth coverage for over 2,860 publications, with more than 1,885 available in full text. With ABI/INFORM Global, users can find out about business conditions, management techniques, business trends, management practice and theory, corporate strategy and tactics, and competitive landscape.

Business and Industry published by **RDS®** and the **GaleGroup** contains important facts, figures, and key events dealing with public and private companies, industries, products and markets for all manufacturing and service industries at an international level. Business and Industry focuses on a body of literature that includes leading trade magazines, newsletters, the general business press, and international business dailies.

Business Source Premier provides full text for over 2,710 scholarly business journals covering management, economics, finance, accounting, international business and much more. This database now has **Datamonitor** industry profiles.

HOOVERS™ Online also provides news, business features, lists, stock quotes, and other business information such as Hoover's Industry Snapshots (global industry overviews). Hoover's covers some 14,000 public and private enterprises worldwide.

LexisNexis® accesses over 6,000 news, business, and legal sources. The news coverage includes deep backfiles and up-to-the-minute stories in national and regional newspapers, wire services, broadcast transcripts, international news, and non-English language sources. It includes the Company Dossier module to retrieve detailed company information and financial performance measures. It identifies and compares companies matching specific criteria.

Power Verbs

Your resume should telegraph action and that you get things done. You can use Power Verbs for that purpose. It is important not to repeat the same word over and over again. To assist you in selecting the most appropriate words for your resume, below are dozens of different words that you can select for inclusion in your resume. Remember that one of the most important considerations is that the words in your resume match up with words in an advertised job description.

This is an abbreviated list. Please go to this link to review hundreds of Power Verbs that you may find relevant to your cover letter and resume: www.thesecrettogettingajobaftercollege.com/powerverbs.html

Accelerated	Chaired	Explained
Accomplished	Circulated	Extracted
Achieved	Classified	Fabricated
Acquainted	Cleared	Followed up
Acquired	Combined	Fomented
Activated	Compared	Found
Added	Compiled	Furthered
Addressed	Completed	Gained
Administered	Complied	Governed
Appointed	Cultivated	Graded
Approached	Demonstrated	Granted
Approved	Depreciated	Handled
Arbitrated	Described	Headed
Articulated	Diagnosed	Helped
Assembled	Disbursed	Hired
Assessed	Documented	Hosted
Audited	Doubled	Identified
Authored	Downsized	Implemented
Authorized	Drafted	Improved
Awarded	Economized	Increased
Balanced	Edited	Innovated
Billed	Educated	Installed
Boosted	Effected	Insured
Broadened	Established	Interpreted
Budgeted	Estimated	Invested
Capitalized	Expanded	Involved
Captured	Expedited	Isolated
Cataloged	Experimented	Issued

Involved	Pursued	Started
Isolated	Quadrupled	Steered
Issued	Quantified	Stimulated
Joined	Quoted	Strategized
Judged	Raised	Streamlined
Justified	Ran	Strengthened
Launched	Ranked	Stressed
Lectured	Realized	Structured
Listened	Reassured	Studied
Located	Received	Submitted
Motivated	Reclaimed	Substantiated
Multiplied	Recommended	Substituted
Named	Reconciled	Supplied
Narrated	Reconstructed	Supported
Navigated	Recorded	Targeted
Negotiated	Recovered	Taught
Nursed	Recruited	Terminated
Nurtured	Rectified	Tested
Obliged	Rejected	Testified
Observed	Related	Tightened
Obtained	Reorganized	Took
Offered	Repaired	Traced
Offset	Reshaped	Transformed
Opened	Resolved	Translated
Operated	Responded	Tripled
Overhauled	Retained	Tutored
Oversaw	Retrieved	Typed
Packaged	Revamped	Uncovered
Patterned	Revealed	Undertook
Penalized	Reversed	Underwrote
Perceived	Saved	Unearthed
Persuaded	Scheduled	Unified
Phased out	Served	Utilized
Piloted	Serviced	Validated
Placed	Signed	Valued
Planned	Spread	Visited
Provided	Stabilized	Witnessed
Publicized	Staffed	Won
Published	Staged	Worked

BIBLIOGRAPHY

Most of these books have been identified through a review of the books available from the bookstore associated with the National Association of Colleges and Employers (NACE). These books are considered very helpful to college graduates as they plan their careers and their lives.

Arruda, William and Dixson, Kirsten. Career Distinction: Stand Out by Building Your Brand. 2007.

Asher, Donald. How to Get Any Job with Any Major: A New Look at Career Launch. 2004.

Barro, Arlene R. Win Without Competing!: Career Success the Right Fit Way (Capital Ideas for Business & Personal Development). 2007.

Bolles, Richard N. What Color is Your Parachute. 2010.

Bolles, Mark E. and Bolles, Richard N. Job-Hunting Online. 2008.

Brooks, Katherine. You Majored in What?: Mapping Your Path From Chaos to Career. 2009.

Bustamente, Gerald G. From College to Career: Making a Successful Transition to the Corporate World. 2007.

Campbell, David. If You Don't Know Where You're Going, You'll Probably End Up Somewhere Else: Finding a Career and Getting a Life. 2007.

Cassio, Jim and Rush, Alice. Green Careers: Choosing Work for a Sustainable Future. 2009.

Combs, Patrick. Major in Success: Make College Easier, Fire Up Your Dreams, and Get a Great Job. 2007.

Coplin, William. 10 Things Employers Want You to Learn in College: The Know-How You Need to Succeed. 2003.

Dawson, Sheryl and Dawson, Kenneth. Job Search: The Total System (3rd Ed). 2008.

DeCarlo, Lauren and Guarneri, Susan. Job Search Bloopers: Every Mistake You Can Make on the Road to Career Suicide.and How to Avoid Them. 2008.

Demarais, Ann, and White, Valerie. First Impressions: What You Don't Know About How Others See You. 2005.

Dikel, Margaret and Roehm, Frances. Guide to Internet Job Searching 2008-2009. 2008.

Dunning, Donna. What's Your Type of Career?: Unlock the Secrets of Your Personality to Find Your Perfect Career Path. 2001.

Fader, Christine. Career Cupid: Your Guide to Landing and Loving Your Dream Job. 2009.

Freedman, Elizabeth. Work 101: Learning the Ropes of the Workplace without Hanging Yourself. 2007.

Freud, Zelda. My Work Book: How to Find a Job - Even During Tough Times - And Survive Your First Year in the Workplace. 2009.

Ferrazzi, Keith and Raz, Tahl. Never Eat Alone: And Other Secrets to Success, One Relationship at a Time. 2005.

Graham, Shawn. Courting Your Career: Match Yourself With the Perfect Job. 2007.

Greene, Brenda. You've Got the Interview Now What?: Fortune 500 Hiring Professionals Tell You How to Get Hired. 2005.

Gregory, Michael. The Career Chronicles: An Insider's Guide to What Jobs Are Really Like - the Good, the Bad, and the Ugly from Over 750 Professionals. 2008.

Hachey, Jean-Marc. The Big Guide To Living And Working Overseas: 3,045 Career Building Resources (Fourth Edition with CD-ROM). 2004.

Hansen, Katharine. A Foot in the Door: Networking Your Way into the Hidden Job Market. 2008.

Hayden, C.J. and Traditi, Frank. Get Hired Now! A 28-Day Program for Landing the Job You Want. 2005.

Kennedy, Susan and Baker, Karen. The Job Coach for Young Professionals: The Workbook for Landing the Right Job. 2009.

Kessler, Robin. Competency-Based Interviews: Master the Tough New Interview Style And Give Them the Answers That Will Win You the Job. 2006.

Kessler, Robin and Strasburg, Linda A. Competency-Based Resumes: How To Bring Your Resume To The Top Of The Pile. 2004.

Lakstins, Daniel www.thirtycareers.com

Lerner, Dick. Dress Like the Big Fish: How to Achieve the Image You Want and the Success You Deserve. 2008.

Liptak, John. Career Quizzes: 12 Tests to Help You Discover and Develop Your Dream Career. 2008.

Lore, Nicholas. Now What? The Young Person's Guide to Choosing the Perfect Career. 2008.

Matias, Linda. How to Say It Job Interviews. 2007.

Pierson, Orville. Highly Effective Networking: Meet the Right People and Get a Great Job. 2009.

Pink, Daniel H. A Whole New Mind: Why Right-Brainers Will Rule the Future. 2006.

Pollak, Lindsey. Getting from College to Career: 90 Things to Do Before You Join the Real World. 2007.

Ryan, Daniel J. Job Search Handbook for People With Disabilities. 2004.

Ryan, Robin. Soaring on Your Strengths: Discover, Use, and Brand Your Best Self for Career Success. 2005.

Schonberger, Chris. Gradspot.com's Guide to Life After College (2009/2010 Edition). 2009.

Shellhart, Joyce Nelson. Dress to Impress: How a Navy Blazer Changed My Life! 2004.

Skillings, Pamela. Escape from Corporate America: A Practical Guide to Creating the Career of Your Dreams. 2008.

Weddle, Peter. Work Strong: Your Personal Career Fitness System. 2009.

Whiteman, Lily. How to Land a Top-Paying Federal Job: Your Complete Guide to Opportunities, Internships, Resumes and Cover Letters, Application Essays (KSAs), Interviews, Salaries, Promotions and More! 2008.

Wiskup, Mark. The It Factor: Be the One People Like, Listen to, and Remember. 2007.

Zeiss, Tony. Build Your Own Ladder: 4 Secrets to Making Your Career Dreams Come True. 2006.

Zichy, Shoya, and Bidou, Ann. Career Match: Connecting Who You Are with What You'll Love to Do. 2007.

Source Notes

CHAPTER ONE

Page 13
Personal Branding Tips for Students
http://www.naceweb.org/so09292010/student_branding/

Page 18
Tom Rath. StrengthFinder 2.0, Gallup Press, 2007.

Page 26
Peter Drucker. How to be an Employee, *Psychology Today*, Vol. 10, March 1968, Pages 63-69.

Page 28-30
Best Jobs in America
http://money.cnn.com/magazines/moneymag/bestjobs/2009

CareerCast
http://www.careercast.com/jobs/content/JobsRated_10BestJobs

Page 33
Linda Kaplan Thaler and Robin Koval. The Power of Nice: How to Conquer the Business World with   Kindness Broadway Books, 2006.

Page 41-42
Sarah Needleman. Experts Weigh in on Job Boards, *The Wall Street Journal*, 02/17/2009.

CHAPTER TWO

Page 47-48
Jared Sandberg.   Short Hours, Big Pay And Other Little Lies
From Your Future Boss, *The Wall Street Journal*
(Eastern Edition), 10/22/2003, Vol. 242 Issue 80, pB1-B1, 2p, 1

Page 50
Steven R. Covey. *The Seven Habits of Highly Effective People*, Free
Press, 1989.

Page 70
Lisa Parker. How to Write a Value Based Resume.
http://www.helium.com/items/1182642-how-to-write-a-resume

Page 102

Emily Steel and Geoffrey A. Fowler. Facebook in Privacy Breach,
The Wall Street Journal, 10/18/2010.

Geoffrey A. Fower and Emily Steel. MySpace, Apps Leak User
Data to Advertisers, *The Wall Street Journal*, 10/23/2010.

Page 105-106

Lonny Strum. 10 Ways to Unlock the Power of LinkedIn.

http://ezinearticles.com/?10-Ways-to-Unlock-the-Power-of-
LinkedIn&id=5140773

CHAPTER THREE

Page 127
Malcolm Gladwell. Blink: The Power of Thinking
Without Thinking, Little, Brown and Company, 2005.

Page 127
Janine Willis, Alexander Todorov. First Impressions: Making Up Your Mind After a 100-Ms Exposure to a Face *Psychological Science*, Vol. 17, No. 7, 2006, Pages 592 - 598.

Page 149-150

Marat Gaziev. I Asserted Myself, and Got the Job, *The New York Times*, 10/30/2010

CHAPTER FOUR

Page 172
Stanford University
http://news.stanford.edu/news/2005/june15/jobs-061505.html

About the Author

Larry Chiagouris has been called "a branding guru", an "All-Star marketing strategist", and "a consumer behavior expert" by the media. His opinions on modern marketing practice have appeared in hundreds of media outlets throughout the world, including the *Today Show*, *Fox News*, and *The Wall Street Journal*. He has authored more than 50 articles and books including *Branding on the Internet*, one of the first articles addressing the Internet and the branding of products. He is one of the few marketing executives who, over the course of a career, has held senior positions in advertising, public relations, and Internet marketing.

He currently holds an appointment at the Lubin School of Business of Pace University in New York as a Professor of Marketing where his interest in the topics of personal branding and career development were first developed. He has lectured to thousands of students and executives for more than 25 years on best practices in marketing and advertising.

He began his career at AT&T, collaborating with Bell Labs scientists to accelerate its innovations. He has held executive positions at Silicon Valley startup eCode.com, the Starz Encore Media Group and major consulting, advertising and public relations agencies, including BrandMarketing Services, Creamer Dickson Basford, Grey Advertising, Bozell, and Backer Spielvogel Bates Advertising. His extensive business experience spans both senior client and marketing services assignments. He has been responsible for creating marketing programs for leading brands, including Avis, Brut, Campbell Soup, Fruit of the Loom, Kool-Aid, Panasonic, Pfizer, Pizza Hut, Prudential, Skippy, Snickers, Vanity Fair, and Visa. He has contributed to the development of some of the most memorable marketing campaigns of the past 20 years, including what may be the longest running print campaign in America, the Milk Moustache campaign.

He received a B.S. in Economics, Magna cum Laude and an A.P.C. in Marketing from New York University. He holds an M.Phil in Business, an M.B.A. in Industrial Psychology, and a Ph.D. in Marketing and Consumer Behavior from the City University of New York. He has served as a member of the Board of Directors of the American Marketing Association and as Chairman of the Advertising Research Foundation.

He is a member of the Marketing Executives Networking Group, the American Association of Public Opinion Research, and the National Association of Colleges and Employers.

CPSIA information can be obtained at www.ICGtesting.com
Printed in the USA
LVOW101704130212

268493LV00011B/152/P